FOURTH GRADE

SCHOLASTIC

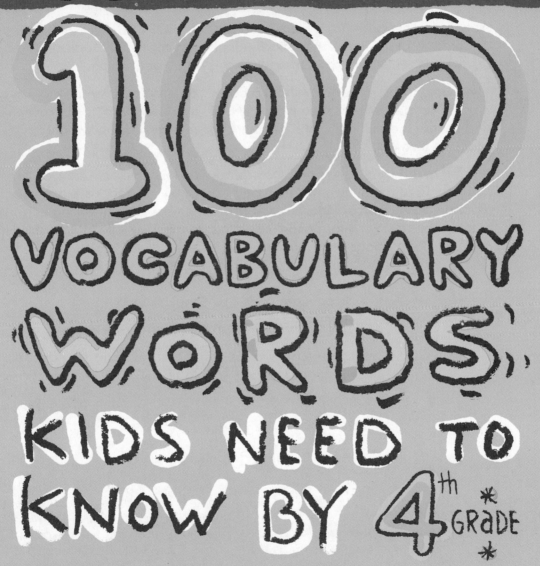

100 VOCABULARY WORDS KIDS NEED TO KNOW BY 4th GRADE

SCHOLASTIC INC.

New York   Toronto   London   Auckland   Sydney
Mexico City   New Delhi   Hong Kong   Buenos Aires

Editor: Sheila Keenan
Art Director: Nancy Sabato
Assistant Designer: Kristen Ekeland
Managing Editor: Karyn Browne
Production Editor: Bonnie Cutler
Project Management: Kevin Callahan, BNGO Books
Composition: Kevin Callahan, Patty Harris, Tony Lee, Daryl Richardson

Copyeditor/Proofreader: Geraldine Albert, Abigail Winograd
Cover: Red Herring Design
Editorial Consultant: Mary C. Rose, Orange County Public Schools, Orlando, Florida
Activity Pages Writer: Kama Einhorn
Activity Pages Illustrator: Laura Huliska-Beith

Dictionary entries are from the *SCHOLASTIC CHILDREN'S DICTIONARY*, New and Updated. Published by Scholastic Reference, an imprint of Scholastic Inc. Copyright © 2002, 1996 by Scholastic Inc. Used by permission.

ISBN 0-439-56676-2

12 11 10 9 8 7 6 5 4 3 2 1   4 5 6 7 8 9/0

Printed in the U.S.A.   40

First printing, January, 2004

Dear Family Member,

Your fourth grader already has quite a large vocabulary, which he or she has acquired indirectly, by watching television, videos, and movies, by listening to and talking with adults and other children, and by reading a variety of materials. Scholastic's *100 Vocabulary Words Kids Need to Know by 4th Grade* will provide *direct* instruction for increasing your child's vocabulary—and for improving reading, writing, and testing skills.

The 100 words in this workbook are words that fourth graders encounter frequently. These words help children expand their vocabularies through word building. And linguists estimate that for every new word children learn, they actually incorporate six or seven other words into their vocabulary in the process.

You are an important part of that process. As your fourth grader moves through the fun and engaging activities in this workbook, you may want to

- Read the dictionary pages at the beginning of each word group together. Talk about familiar situations in which you might use these words. Doing this helps your child understand word meanings and learn them quicker.

- Offer to help your child with a few pages at the beginning of each word group until he or she becomes familiar with the words in that group.

- Ask your child to read out loud. Reading out loud helps a child gain fluency and confidence and learn the correct pronunciation of unfamiliar words. Be sure to give your child time to listen to himself or herself and self-correct.

- Spelling counts in learning new words. Help your child look for spelling patterns that he or she already knows.

- Use some of these 100 words in everyday conversation with your child.

- Encourage your fourth grader to read, read, read!

We've included a set of fun bookmarks with vocabulary strategies and dictionary tips for your child to use when reading—because that's what vocabulary development is all about: building strong readers!

Jean Feiwel
Scholastic Publisher, Senior Vice President

A Note About the 100 Words

The 100 words in this book were carefully chosen from master word lists developed by educators and linguists. For ease of use, we have provided definitions from our *Scholastic Children's Dictionary.* In some cases, the word from the 100 Words list appears near or at the end of the definition of its root word rather than as its own entry. For example, *curiosity,* from Word Group 1, appears near the end of the definition for *curious* on page 7.

My 100 Words

Group 1

abandon

ability

abroad

agreeable

brief

budge

confuse

convenient

curiosity

descend

Group 2

deserve

disappointment

disaster

discover

emerge

encourage

enthusiasm

explanation

exploration

express

Group 3

extraordinary

extreme

fascinate

formal

fortunate

frantic

frequent

furious

generation

gesture

Group 4

glimpse

grief

hesitate

impress

increase

independent

ingredient

innocent

inquire

inspire

Group 5

involve

launch

loyal

manufacture

massive

migrate

mischief

mission

navigate

neglect

Group 6

observe	original
occasion	permanent
official	plunge
opinion	possess
opportunity	pounce

Group 7

preserve	purchase
proceed	quarrel
produce	recover
prompt	reflect
publish	relation

Group 8

release	scarce
represent	seize
request	shatter
reveal	solution
satisfy	source

Group 9

stagger	terrify
support	territory
suspicious	thorough
switch	threaten
tackle	tradition

Group 10

tread	volunteer
triumph	weary
union	wisdom
urgent	wreck
vast	wring

Contents

Dive Into the Dictionary! The words in a dictionary are in alphabetical order. This means the first words begin with the letter **a**; the second section of words all begin with **b**, and so on.

a·ban·don (uh-**ban**-duhn) *verb*
1. To leave forever. *Abandon ship!*
2. To give up. *Never abandon hope!*
▷ *verb* **abandoning, abandoned**

a·bil·i·ty (uh-**bil**-i-tee) *noun*
1. The power to do something. *I know I have the ability to do better.*
2. Skill. *Pablo has great ability in art.*
▷ *noun, plural* **abilities**

a·broad (uh-**brawd**) *adverb* In or to another country. In the United States, *abroad* usually means "overseas." *We are going abroad this fall.*

a·gree·a·ble (uh-**gree**-uh-buhl) *adjective*
1. Pleasing or likable. *Ken is an agreeable person.*
2. Willing or ready to say yes. *If you are agreeable, we will meet an hour before the show.*

brief (**breef**)
1. *adjective* Lasting only a short time, as in *a brief visit.*
2. *adjective* Using only a few words. *Be as brief as you can.*
3. *verb* To give someone information so that the person can carry out a task. *The sales manager briefed her staff on the new products.* ▷ **briefing, briefed**
4. *noun* An outline of the main information and arguments of a legal case.
▷ *adjective* **briefer, briefest**
▷ *adverb* **briefly**

budge (**buhj**) *verb* If you cannot **budge** something, you are not able to move it.
▷ **budging, budged**

con·fuse (kuhn-**fyooz**) *verb*
1. If someone or something **confuses** you, you do not understand it or know what to do. ▷ *adjective* **confusing, confused**
2. To mistake one thing for another. *I confused Roy with his twin brother.*
▷ *verb* **confusing, confused**
▷ *noun* **confusion**

con·ven·ient (kuhn-**vee**-nyuhnt) **adjective** If something is **convenient,** it is useful or easy to use. *The No. 4 bus is very convenient for me since it stops right near my house.* ▷ *adverb* **conveniently**

cu·ri·ous (**kyur**-ee-uhss) *adjective*
1. Eager to find out.
2. Strange, as in *a curious creature.*
▷ *noun* **curiosity** (kyur-ee-**ahss**-i-tee)
▷ *adverb* **curiously**

de·scend (di-**send**) *verb*
1. To climb down or go down to a lower level. *To get downstairs, you will need to descend the staircase.*
2. If you are **descended** from someone, you belong to a later generation of the same family.
▷ *verb* **descending, descended**
▷ *noun* **descent**

Use one of the 10 words defined above to finish this rhyme.

The great boxer Muhammad Ali once said,
"Float like a butterfly, sting like a bee."

He could do it, because he had _____!

Which Word Am I?

Read the description. Choose from the words in the box.
Then write the answer on the line.

Word Box

abandon	abroad	brief	confuse	curiosity
ability	agreeable	budge	convenient	descend

I have 3 syllables.
I mean the opposite of "to stay."
I mean the same as "to leave."
I am a verb.

_____

I have 4 syllables.
My root word is **able**.
My suffix **-ity** tells you that I am a noun.

_____

I have 2 syllables.
I am the opposite of "home."
I mean the same as "far away."
I rhyme with **clawed**.

_____

I have 4 syllables.
I am the opposite of "cranky."
I mean the same as "good-natured."

_____

I have 1 syllable.
I am the opposite of "long."
I mean the same as "short."
I am used to describe a period of time.

_____

I have 1 syllable. I have 2 vowels.
I am often found after the words
would not.
I mean the same as "move."
I rhyme with **fudge**.

_____

I have 2 syllables.
I am the opposite of "make clear."
I mean the same as "mix up."
I rhyme with **blues**.

_____

I have 3 syllables.
I am the opposite of "hassle."
I mean the same as "easy."

_____

I have 5 syllables.
I am the opposite of "disinterested."
My suffix **-ity** tells you that I am a noun.

_____

I have 2 syllables.
I am the opposite of "to go up."
I mean the same as "to go down."
I rhyme with **pretend**.

_____

What a Combination!

Read each sentence. Then choose the right word from the box to complete it.

Word Box

| ability | able | curiosity | curious |

My cat has 2 qualities that, together, equal disaster!

These 2 traits are _____ and _____ .

First of all, since cats have the _____ to climb very high, my pet can

really get into some interesting places. She is even _____ to get

on top of bookshelves. She is also _____ to climb a tree, but she is

not always _____ to get down by herself!

Second, my cat is so _____ . She always wants to see what's in

the trees, over the fence, or inside a bag. She is full of _____ ! Her

_____ knows no bounds. She has a natural

_____ to smell things, too. That means she knows if we bring

home groceries that include fish. Then she meows until we give her a treat.

My cat was also born with the _____ to hunt. She is always

chasing bugs and birds. Some cats don't have much _____ .

Very little interests them—they just like to sleep all day. Not my cat! If you have a pet

like mine, full of _____ and _____ , you've got

your hands full!

Hink Pinks

Hink Pinks are riddles with rhyming answers. Read the riddles, and choose from the words in the box to write the answers.

Word Box

abroad	brief	chief	convenient	mint
applaud	budge	confuse	fudge	shoes

What do you do when you put your sneakers on the wrong feet?

_____ your

_____

What do you call a candy that's always there when you need it?

A _____ _____

What do you call a president who is only in office for one day?

A _____ _____

What do you call chocolate that sticks to the pan?

_____ that won't _____

What do you do when you clap at a concert overseas?

You _____ _____.

Pyramid Power

Read the clues. Then fill in a word from the box at the pyramid top.
Use that word in a sentence underneath the pyramid.

Hint: An **antonym** is
a word's opposite.

Word Box

abandon   abroad

ability   confuse

Hint: A **synonym**
is a word with a
meaning similar
to another word.

1

antonym: **clarify**
synonyms: **mix up,
befuddle**

2

antonym: **stay**
synonyms: **give up, leave**

3

antonym: **inability**
synonyms: **skill, talent**

4

antonym: **at home**
synonyms: **overseas, faraway**

Mixed-up Messages

Dear Ms. Jones,

   I am writing this letter to let you know I am very interested in your company, Europe, Incorporated, and would like a job working abroad. I have the ability to speak many languages, and am curious about foreign cultures. I love traveling, seeing new sights, and meeting people from different cultures.

   If it is convenient, I would like to set up a brief meeting to talk with you about my work experience. I am agreeable to an early-morning or evening meeting.

Sincerely,

Mr. Smith

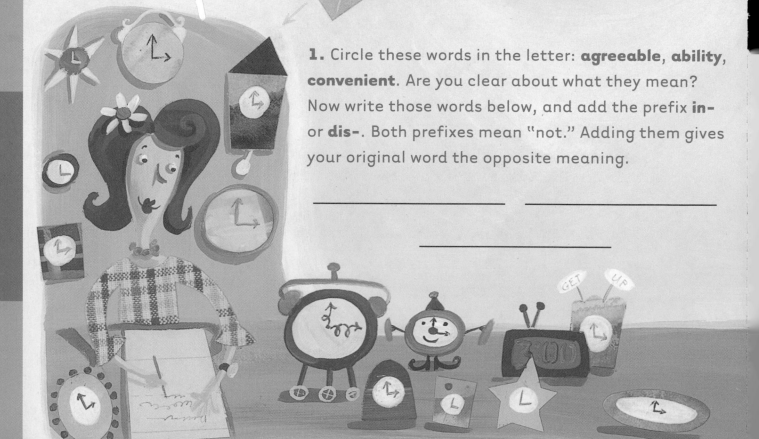

1. Circle these words in the letter: **agreeable**, **ability**, **convenient**. Are you clear about what they mean? Now write those words below, and add the prefix **in-** or **dis-**. Both prefixes mean "not." Adding them gives your original word the opposite meaning.

_____   _____

_____

Dear Mr. Smith,

Thank you for your letter. Your skills sound impressive. But I'm afraid you are confused. Our name is not Europe, Incorporated. Nor are we an international company. Our company is You're Up, Incorporated. We sell alarm clocks in a small store on a small street in a small town in a small state.

If you are still interested in working for our alarm company, give us a loud ring.

Sincerely,

Ms. Jones

2. Circle these words in the letter: **confused**, **curious**. Add the suffix **-ity** or **-ion**. Hint: You may have to change the spelling to add a suffix.

_____   _____

3. Now use the 4 words from above to complete the sentences. When you're finished, circle the nouns you wrote, and underline the **adjectives** (describing words).

Mr. Smith was _____ about a company he thought was

international. His _____ led him to write Ms. Jones a letter.

Mr. Smith was _____ about the company. His

_____ was due to a misunderstanding about the

company's name.

Some words can't take suffixes or prefixes. Find the word in the story that means the same as the highlighted word. Write it on the line.

Mr. Smith would like to work **overseas**. _____

Captain Wanted

Use the words from the box to complete the sentences.

Word Box

abandon	abroad	brief	convenient
ability	agreeable	confuse	curiosity

Ten sailors need a good captain to lead exciting adventures around the world. The right person for the job is a good leader who knows the ocean. Must be willing to _____ home to sail _____. _____ about different countries and cultures is a plus. Must have the _____ to steer and predict weather. Must be able to tolerate only _____ visits to land. Must never _____ north and south. Most of all, must be cheerful and _____. It would be _____ if you are from our hometown, so we don't have to make an extra stop when we go ashore to visit our families. Apply in person at the city dock. Look for the ten sailors hanging around their ship.

Antonyms Attract

Draw lines to match each word with its **antonym**.

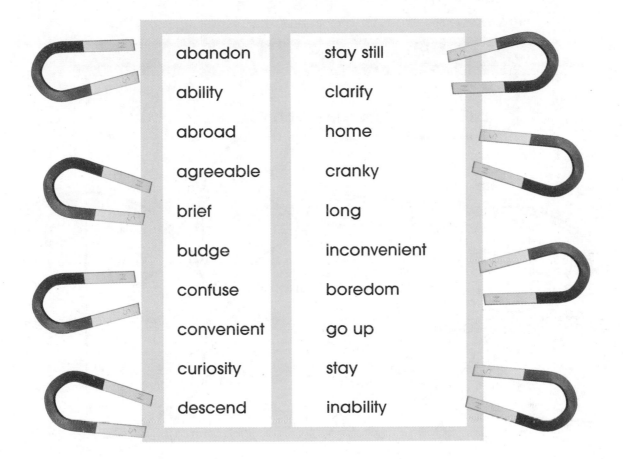

abandon	stay still
ability	clarify
abroad	home
agreeable	cranky
brief	long
budge	inconvenient
confuse	boredom
convenient	go up
curiosity	stay
descend	inability

Describe something you do every day that is **convenient**:
Do you shop at a certain store? go to a certain bus stop?
know a shortcut home?

_____

_____

Now describe something you have to do that is **inconvenient**.

_____

_____

Spinning Synonyms

Each bike wheel has a word missing. Read all the **synonyms** in each wheel.
(You don't need to know the meaning of each one to complete the wheel.)
Find the word from the box that fits. Write it in the space.

Word Box

abandon	abroad	brief	convenient
ability	agreeable	confuse	curious

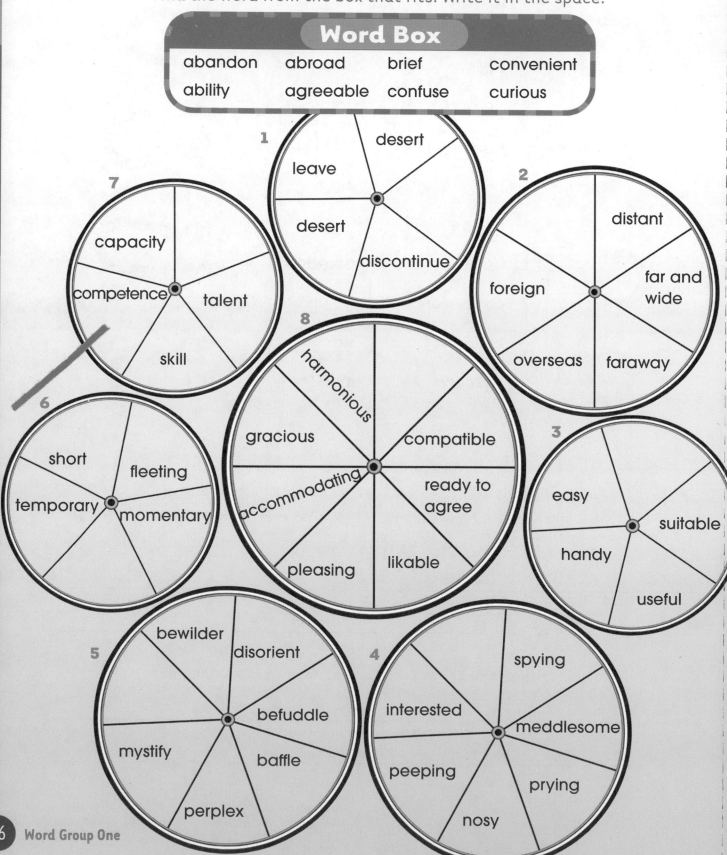

1
desert
leave
desert
discontinue

7
capacity
competence
talent
skill

2
distant
foreign
far and wide
overseas
faraway

8
harmonious
gracious
compatible
accommodating
ready to agree
pleasing
likable

6
short
fleeting
temporary
momentary

3
easy
suitable
handy
useful

5
bewilder
disorient
befuddle
mystify
baffle
perplex

4
spying
interested
meddlesome
peeping
prying
nosy

Presto Change-O!

By changing a word's ending, you keep the big idea but change the way the word is used. Nouns can change into verbs, adjectives can change into nouns, and so on. For example, *I put the cookies in a* **container** *(noun).* *The cookie jar* **contains** *(verb) the cookies.*

Word Box

abandon	agreement	convenience
ability	confuse	curiosity

descend

Change these **nouns** (naming words) into **verbs** (action words). Choose from the words in the box.

Noun	Verb	Noun	Verb
confusion	_____	abandonment	_____
descent	_____		

Use one of these noun/verb word pairs to finish these sentences.

The dance class was full of _____. Some students were

_____ about whether to go left or go right.

Change these **adjectives** (describing words) into **nouns** (naming words). Choose from the words in the box.

Adjective	Noun	Adjective	Noun
able	_____	convenient	_____
agreeable	_____	curious	_____

Use one of these adjective/noun word pairs to finish these sentences.

"_____ killed the cat" is an old saying. It means you can

sometimes get in trouble by being too _____.

Word History

Many English words come from Latin, an ancient language. Read the words in the left column, then draw a line to match each word to its origin.

budge	From the Latin word *habilitas*, which means "aptitude or handy."
convenient	From the Latin word *brevis*, which means "short." (Later, Middle English used the word *bref* to mean the same thing.)
descend	From *gratum* in Latin, which means "something agreeable." Later, it developed into the Old French phrase *à gré*, which means "at pleasure."
ability	From the Anglo-French word *bouger*, meaning "to stir or move slightly."
confuse	From the Latin *confusus*, meaning "mixed."
agreeable	From the Latin *conveniere*, meaning "to come together, be suitable."
brief	From the Latin *descendere*, meaning "to climb down." (*Scend* means "climb.")

Different Ways to Descend

Choose from the words in the box to complete each sentence.
Words can be used more than once.

Word Box

descend   descendant descended descent

To move from a higher to lower place is to _____.

To get to the basement, you must _____ the staircase.

A helicopter can _____ right onto a rooftop.

After reaching the top of the mountain, the climbers began to _____.

The plane began its _____.

You can see all the _____s of the oldest

person on the tree. His father, grandfather, and great-grandfather were all royalty.

He is _____ from a long line of kings. His _____s,

his son, grandson, and great-grandson, will also be kings.

Conveniently Convenient

Read each sentence, and complete it with a word from the box.
You can use one of the words more than once.

Word Box

convenience
convenience food
convenience store

convenient
conveniently

A bus stop right in front of your house makes traveling around very

_____. It is very _____ located.

The new apartment has all the latest modern _____s:
dishwasher, microwave, and refrigerator with a built-in ice maker!

Having a fold-out couch is very _____ if you have sleep-over guests.

A _____ _____ is a shop where you can find lots

of different things: food, drugstore items, magazines, and candy.

A frozen dinner that is quick and easy to fix is

called a _____ _____.

All About Me

Read each sentence.
Circle **YES** or **NO** to tell
about yourself.

I would like to adopt an abandoned animal.	YES	NO
I would like to travel abroad.	YES	NO
I like to take brief naps after school.	YES	NO
When I have a strong opinion and someone is trying to change my mind, I usually won't budge.	YES	NO
I am generally an agreeable person.	YES	NO
My curioslty about outer space could lead me to become an astronaut.	YES	NO

Complete the sentences.

My curiosity about

_____

_____

If I could travel anywhere abroad, it would be to _____ because

_____

_____.

We MEAN it!

SCRAM!

GET OUT!

No TRESPASSING

BEWARE

That Spooky Old House

One day, Jim walked home from school a different way. He passed an old, spooky house. It looked as if it had been abandoned for years. Shutters hung lopsided from their frames. The paint was chipped and peeled. Grass and weeds choked the front yard.

Who owned this house? Why was it deserted? Jim had heard all sorts of stories about the place. That very morning, his friend Miguel had told him the place was haunted by a rich old man who had died inside the house, counting his money. At lunch, Jim's friend Brian had told him big black bats roosted there . . . *vampire* bats. Brian said they swooped out at night, looking for something—or someone—to bite! Jim didn't know what to think about the house. These tales were all so confusing!

That afternoon, as Jim passed by the old house, he spotted two shadows flitting across the upstairs window. Jim's curiosity grew. Were they bat's wings? Or an old man's hands full of money? Jim had to find out. He turned in and headed up the front steps.

At first the door didn't budge. Jim pushed harder. The door slowly creaked open. Jim stepped inside. Darkness descended on him like a heavy blanket. He could barely see.

"Hello?" Jim called. The wind carried his voice, stretching the o to an OOOOOOO.

"Helloooooo!" Jim called again.

"Hellooooooo!" a voice called back.

A ghost? A vampire? Jim didn't care anymore. He raced outside and didn't look back. Just as suddenly, two figures shot out through the side door of the house. They ran off in the other direction.

Jim raced around the corner. He was running so fast that he bumped right into Miguel and Brian, who were running toward him from the opposite direction. All three friends started talking at once.

"I was in the old house," Jim said.

"We were, too," said Miguel and Brian.

"I heard a ghost," Jim continued.

"We did, too," Miguel and Brian chimed in.

"It said . . ." Jim began.

". . . Helloooooooo!" Miguel and Brian finished.

"How did you know?" Jim asked. The three friends stared at each other. Then they burst out laughing.

"What a fine set of ghosts we make," said Miguel.

"Well, we looked pale enough a minute ago to be the real thing!" laughed Jim.

Number the sentences below from 1 to 10 to show the order
in which things happened in the story.

_____ Jim tried to push the door, but it wouldn't budge.

_____ Jim, Miguel, and Brian realized it was each other they had heard
in the old house.

_____ Jim became even more curious after he saw the shadows.

_____ Jim walked past a spooky, deserted house.

_____ Jim felt the darkness descend on him like a heavy blanket.

_____ Jim thinks back to what Miguel and Brian had told him about
the house being haunted by an old man or vampire bats.

_____ Two figures ran out of the side door of the house.

_____ Jim heard someone—or something—call hello.

_____ Jim ran out of the house.

_____ Jim called hello.

Name It!

Each thing below needs a name. Circle the correct name for each. Then write a short sentence explaining why you chose the name you did.

A city where everything is interesting: Curiosity, USA or Blah Town?

Why? _____

A restaurant far away where nothing ever goes right and the food is always late:
The Convenient Café or Hamburger Hassle?

Why? _____

A travel agency specializing in exciting travel:
Adventure Abroad, Inc. or The Couch Potato Company?

Why? _____

A street with no cars or people: Crowded Crossing or Abandoned Alley?

Why? _____

A scuba tour company that leads deep-sea scuba trips:
Descend Diving Company or Fly-Away Tours?

Why? _____

A new computer model that promises to work really fast:
The Endless 3000 or Brief 3000?

Why? _____

A tow truck company that will pull your car out of the mud:
Budge Brothers or Stay Stuck, Inc.?

Why? _____

A store in a basement: The Antique Attic or Descend 'n' Spend?

Why? _____

Sort It Out

All the words in this box fit into one of two categories: adjectives or verbs.

An **adjective** describes something. A **verb** shows action—something you do.

Tiny, **large**, **short**, and **long** are all adjectives. **Go**, **play**, **remember**, and **fly** are all verbs.

Write each word from the box in the correct crate.

Verbs (action words)

_____

_____

_____

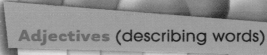

Adjectives (describing words)

_____

_____

_____

Use one of the **verbs** in a sentence.

_____

_____

_____

Use one of the **adjectives** in a sentence.

_____

_____

Bubble Test

Read each question. Fill in the bubble next to the correct answer.

Which situation could you NOT use the word **descend** to describe?
- ○ Going down stairs
- ○ An airplane landing
- ○ Rain coming down
- ○ An airplane taking off
- ○ A mountain climber coming down a mountain after reaching the top

What is NOT **convenient**?
- ○ A store with fast checkout
- ○ A parking lot close to where you're going
- ○ Buses that run every 5 minutes
- ○ A traffic jam
- ○ A small tool kit that fits in your pocket

Which is NOT a synonym for **agreeable**?
- ○ Flexible
- ○ Crabby
- ○ Easygoing
- ○ Cooperative
- ○ Pleasant

Which of the following does NOT seem **brief**?
- ○ A minute
- ○ A long, boring movie
- ○ A TV commercial
- ○ A quick walk
- ○ A second

Which place is NOT **abroad**?
- ○ Taiwan
- ○ France
- ○ China
- ○ Massachusetts
- ○ Egypt

E-mail

Help complete this E-mail. Choose from the words in the box.

To: Tyler Green
From: Sam Smith
Re: Greetings from Italy!

Hi Tyler,

Guess what! I am able to send E-mail from _____. My family

and I arrived in Italy yesterday. We have been very busy, but now I have a

_____ opportunity to use the E-mail in the hotel. I was so sad to

leave home, especially when we had to leave Fluffy with the dog-sitter. I felt like

we were _____ing her! She sat in the car and would not

_____—we had to carry her in.

Italy is really neat. The restaurants are definitely satisfying all my _____

about Italian food and how it is different from the Italian restaurant at home. I took

a cool picture when the plane started to _____. I saw mountains

and the ocean next to a big city. I love Italy! It is a little _____ to

not be able to speak the language, though. I get everything mixed up.

Longer letter later,

Sam

Day Planner

Fill in this weekly schedule.
Choose from the words in the box.

Word Box

ability	budge
abroad	confuse
agreeable	convenient
brief	

Monday — Spend 30 minutes outside improving my _____ to jump rope.

Tuesday — Write a letter to Grandma in Mexico. Remember to use

airmail stamps to send it _____.

Wednesday — Try to be _____ when Dad asks me to do the weekly vacuuming.

Thursday — _____ meeting at clubhouse at 4:00.
(When we vote on what color to paint it, remember

not to _____ on my opinion.)

Friday — Bring books home for homework. Remember to not

_____ my math book with my social studies
book this time. Maybe cover them in different color covers?

Saturday/ Sunday — If _____, ask Mom to swing by the store
to see if they have the new comic books in.

Crossword Puzzle

Use some of the words you learned in Word Group 1 to fill in this puzzle.

Across

1. He's so stubborn, he won't _____.
2. The lawyer prepared a _____.
3. Quick and easy
4. Overseas

Down

5. _____ killed the cat.
6. Leave behind
7. Opposite of "to clear up"

Word Search

Circle these words in the puzzle: **ability**, **abandon**, **abroad**, **agreeable**, **brief**, **budge**, **confuse**, **curious**, **descend**. The words can read across, down, and backward. Hint: They may appear more than once.

```
s b l o o r a x g m k r v u c v q l m n a i b o c e a m x r s t u z d
a g r e e a b l e l s a q b u m n c k b w y j o r a b r o a d f l o e
b b f t o a i p s j w i d d v a g h q u m x c r r y a m c i e k n b s
r c r s a o l c y d l o x a z r w o b d b e n x v l n a r p b i k f c
o t i o m z i r l m e v a x p d s r a g f a b r o a d m v y z g a f e
a v b e a m t w i k m l b r p g o c m e e x a w q n o x t e f c i u n
d e o h g d y o x f b t b y o m v r b a p n e r s t n n e e i o y f d
e s u f n o c r m f i l h a c k a b o t l i z m a s b e i o o f w h x
r s u m o w z p o i l s u x e c o z g v b z i e w l l r t s a b v j n
c o n f u s e v a v w x i l y e g a i x b e i m n p b z u b l r m a n
o p p w i m e s a r y k s u o i r u c a n v x d d i t o r j e e a l o
n o p t n a r i c b a v e r e f s g l e e j n m p u x f d s l a f l d
f i p r a b i l i t y f g x m p s o a l n v h f x d a o r b a u b g n
u p o s w u v c a q f i m l k j w z x m b o d l o g i y c d m s e a a
s l e f h w t x a t l g h u i m n e e x t b r m o r q m p m q x v o b
e l b a e e r g a r r j o h k w i x m o b p u e a c e m h q r e y l a
```

Word Group 1 Answer Key

7 ability

8 abandon, ability, abroad, agreeable, brief, budge, confuse, convenient, curiosity, descend

9 ability/curiosity, ability, able, able, able, curious, curiosity, curiosity, ability, ability, curiosity, ability/curiosity

10 Confuse your shoes, convenient mint, brief chief, Fudge that won't budge, applaud abroad

11 1. confuse, 2. abandon, 3. ability, 4. abroad; answers will vary.

12–13 1. Circle agreeable, ability, convenient; disagreeable, disability/inability, inconvenient; 2. Circle confused, curious; Write confusion, curiosity; 3. curious, curiosity, confused, confusion, international

14 abandon, abroad, Curiosity, ability, brief, confuse, agreeable, convenient

15 abandon/stay, ability/inability, abroad/home, agreeable/cranky, brief/long, budge/stay still, confuse/clarify, convenient/inconvenient, curiosity/boredom, descend/go up

16 1. abandon, 2. abroad, 3. convenient, 4. curious, 5. confuse, 6. brief, 7. ability

17 confuse, descend, abandon; confusion, confused; ability, agreement, convenience, curiosity; Curiosity, curious

18 ability, brief, agreeable, budge, confuse, convenient, descend

19 descend, descend, descend, descend, descent, descendant, descended, descendant

20 convenient, conveniently, convenience, convenient, convenience store, convenience food

21 Answers will vary.

22–23 3, 10, 4, 1, 5, 2, 9, 7, 8, 6

24 Curiosity, USA, Hamburger Hassle, Adventure Abroad, Inc., Abandoned Alley, Descend Diving Company, Brief 3000, Budge Brothers, Descend 'n' Spend; answers will vary.

25 Verbs: budge, confuse, descend, abandon; **Adjectives:** brief, agreeable, convenient; answers will vary.

26 An airplane taking off, A traffic jam, Crabby, A long, boring movie, Massachusetts

27 abroad, brief, abandon, budge, curiosity, descend, confusing

28 ability, abroad, agreeable, Brief, budge, confuse, convenient

29 See answer at right.

30 See answer below.

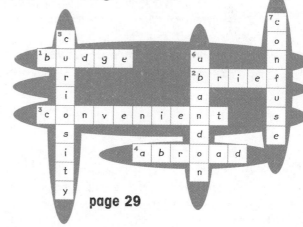

page 29

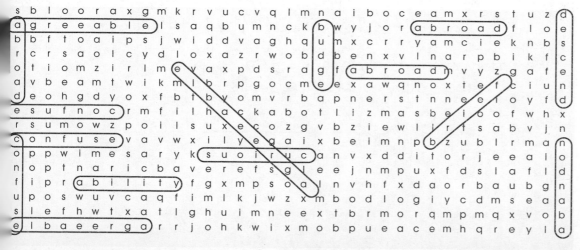

page 30

Dive Into the Dictionary!

Words within a given letter section of the dictionary are also arranged in alphabetical order. You may need to check not only the first letter but the second, third, or more letters to find the word you're looking for.

de·serve (di-**zurv**) *verb* To earn something because of the way you behave. *Angelica deserves a reward for her hard work.*
▷ **deserving, deserved**
▷ *adjective* **deserving**

dis·ap·point (diss-uh-**point**) *verb* To let someone down by failing to do what he or she expected. *George's grades will disappoint his parents.* ▷ **disappointing, disappointed** ▷ *noun* **disappointment**
▷ *adjective* **disappointed, disappointing**

dis·as·ter (duh-**zass**-tur) *noun*
1. An event that causes great damage, loss, or suffering, such as a flood or a serious train wreck.
2. If something is a **disaster**, it turns out completely wrong.
▷ *adjective* **disastrous** ▷ *adverb* **disastrously**

dis·cov·er (diss-**kuh**-vur) *verb*
1. To find something. *We discovered the treasure as we were exploring the attic.*
2. To find out about something. *I soon discovered that Li was lying.*
▷ *verb* **discovering, discovered**
▷ *noun* **discovery,** *noun* **discoverer**

e·merge (i-**murj**) *verb*
1. If you **emerge** from somewhere, you come out into the open.
2. To become known. *News is emerging of a serious avalanche in the mountains.*
▷ *verb* **emerging, emerged**
▷ *noun* **emergence**

en·cour·age (en-**kur**-ij) *verb* To give someone confidence by praising or supporting the person. *The teacher encouraged us to do our best.* ▷ **encouraging, encouraged**
▷ *noun* **encouragement** ▷ *adjective* **encouraging** ▷ *adverb* **encouragingly**

en·thu·si·asm (en-**thoo**-zee-*az*-uhm) *noun* Great excitement or interest. *Tony's speech filled his supporters with enthusiasm.*

ex·plain (ek-**splayn**) *verb*
1. To make something clear so that it is easier to understand. ▷ *adjective* **explanatory** (ek-**splan**-uh-*tor*-ee)
2. To give a reason for something. *Please explain why you are so late.*
▷ *verb* **explaining, explained**
▷ *noun* **explanation** (ex-spluh-**nay**-shuhn)

ex·plo·ra·tion (ek-spluh-**ray**-shuhn) *noun* The act of looking into or studying something or someplace unknown.

ex·press (ek-**spress**)
1. *verb* To show what you feel or think by saying, doing, or writing something. *I express my deepest feelings in my diary.*
▷ **expresses, expressing, expressed**
2. *noun* A fast train or bus that stops at only a few stations. ▷ *noun, plural* **expresses**
3. *adjective* Very fast, as in *express delivery.*

Use one of the 10 words defined above to answer this riddle.

What do you call a hairdo that looks absolutely, unbelievably terrible all by itself?

Answer: A natural _____

Which Word Am I?

Read each description. Then write the correct word on the line. Choose from the words in the box.

Word Box

deserve	encourage
disappointment	enthusiasm
disaster	explanation
discover	exploration
emerge	express

I have 3 syllables.
I am the opposite of "to ignore."
I mean the same as "to find."

_____

I have 4 syllables.
I am the opposite of "excitement."
My suffix **-ment** tells you that I am a noun.

_____

I have 4 syllables.
I am the opposite of "mystery."
I am a synonym for "description."

_____

I have 4 syllables.
My ending **-tion** tells you I am a noun.
My root word ends with an **e**.

_____

I have 2 syllables.
I am the opposite of "to keep secret."
I am a verb.

_____

I have 3 syllables.
I am a terrible thing.
I rhyme with **master**.

_____

I have 3 syllables.
I am the opposite of "to discourage."
I mean the same as "to cheer on."

_____

I have 4 syllables.
I am a noun.
I am a synonym for "interest."

_____

I have 2 syllables.
I am the opposite of "to hide."
I mean the same as "to come out."

_____

I have 2 syllables.
I mean the same as "to be worthy of."
I rhyme with **swerve**.

_____

Action!

The suffix **-ion** or **-tion** is a common word ending.
It means "act of or result of." Any time you see **-ion** or **-tion**
at the end of a word, you know it is a noun.

Examples
A celebration is the act of celebrating.
A separation is the result of being separate.

celebrate   celebration

Complete these 2 sentences using
a word from the box.

Word Box
explanation   exploration

When you explain something, you give an _____.

When you study explorers, you are studying the subject of _____.

Can you think of the **-ion** or **-tion** words that would match these verbs?
Hint: When a verb ends in **e**, drop the **e** before adding **-ion** or **-tion**.
Or you may have to add an **a** or even change a letter. Say the words out loud
before you write them down, to hear how they change.

congregate (to gather) _____   inspect (to look at) _____

inject (to give a shot) _____   confront (to stand up to) _____

describe (to explain) _____   converse (to talk) _____

Explorations & Explanations

The prefix **ex-** is a common word beginning. It means "out of or from." Complete the following sentences. Choose from the words in the box.

Word Box

explain	exploration
explained	explore
explanation	explorer

expressed

expression

It is difficult to _____ how the planets are arranged and how they move, but Mr. Jones gave us a really clear _____ in class. I finally understood how Earth moves around the sun. I went home and _____ it to my little brother.

Space _____ is very interesting to many people. Space _____s are called astronauts. Would you like to _____ outer space?

The astronauts returned to Earth. They _____ their thanks to the people on the ground who had cheered them on. As an _____ of their thanks, they handed out moon rocks to the people in the crowd!

Complete these words. Choose from the root words (basic word parts) in the box.

Word Box

change

port

terminate

to switch: ex_____

to ship goods out of a country: ex_____

to get rid of: ex_____

The Disastrous Discovery

Word Box

disappointment

disaster

discover

discovered

discovery

Dis- is a common prefix. It means "reverse of, or not." So, **discover** means something like "uncover." Complete the following story. Choose from the words in the box.

A scientist decided to invent a chewing gum that would let people blow the biggest bubbles ever. After months in the science lab, she made an amazing

_____. She _____ that if she put a certain combination of chemicals in the gum, it blew up into enormous bubbles.

Her fellow scientists asked, "How did you _____ such a thing? We never would have thought of that."

The scientist was thrilled about her _____. Now all she needed was to test it out on some kids. A friendly principal let the scientist visit a school yard. There, she gave every kid at recess a piece of gum.

"One, 2, 3, blow!" the scientist shouted.

Thirty kids blew thirty gigantic bubbles. They quickly burst. Kids got stuck to each other. Their faces, hands, and hair were full of gum. The playground was coated in a layer of pink, gooey gum. The school-yard experiment was a total

_____!

What a _____! The scientist went back to the lab. "I've got it!" she cried. And she went to work on inventing something new: gum remover!

Synonym Cones

Write the word from the box next to the cone that carries scoops of its **synonyms**, or similar words.

Word Box

deserve	encourage
disappointment	enthusiasm
disaster	explanation
discover	exploration
emerge	express

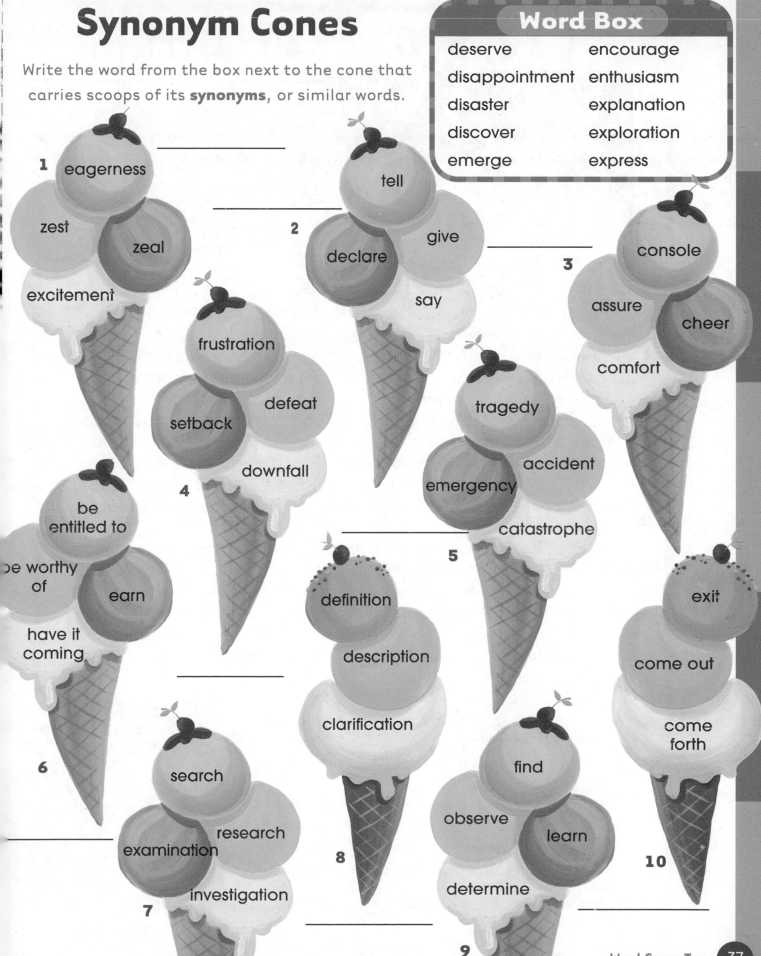

1. _____
eagerness, zest, zeal, excitement

2. _____
tell, give, declare, say

3. _____
console, assure, cheer, comfort

4. _____
frustration, defeat, setback, downfall

5. _____
tragedy, accident, emergency, catastrophe

6. _____
be entitled to, be worthy of, earn, have it coming

7. _____
search, research, examination, investigation

8. _____
definition, description, clarification

9. _____
find, observe, learn, determine

10. _____
exit, come out, come forth

10, 9, 8 . . . Lift Off!

July 16, 1969: The *Apollo 11* blasted into space from Cape Kennedy, Florida. Onboard the spacecraft were three astronauts: Neil Armstrong, Michael Collins, and Edwin "Buzz" Aldrin. The *Apollo 11* was traveling almost 250,000 miles per hour, aiming for a spot almost a quarter of a million miles away—the moon.

The moon travels about 50,000 miles each day in its orbit. Landing on it would require precise calculations. The *Apollo 11*'s flight plan had to be accurate. All nine million pieces of its machinery had to work precisely.

All over the world, people were fascinated by space exploration. They shared the astronauts' dream to discover what's out there, beyond our skies, beyond our knowledge.

Millions of people turned on their TV sets to watch the *Apollo*'s historic flight. Their enthusiasm kept them glued to those screens and wondering: Would *Apollo 11* be the first manned spacecraft to land on the moon? What if something went wrong? At best, there'd be disappointment: no moon landing. At worst, disaster. Everyone was rooting for the astronauts.

July 19: Three days later, the *Apollo 11*'s landing craft dropped onto the moon's surface.

Eureka!

Neil Armstrong, clad in a big, puffy spacesuit, his face hidden by a big helmet, emerged from the hatch. He stepped out . . . and became the man on the moon!

"That's one small step for a man, one giant leap for mankind," Armstrong said. He expressed the feelings of everyone watching. The whole world celebrated this amazing achievement!

Replace the underlined words with their **synonyms**,
which you'll find in the story.

All over the world, people were fascinated by space <u>study</u>. _____

Space travel is inspired by the dream <u>to find out</u> what's out there, beyond our skies,

beyond our knowledge. _____

Millions of people turned on TV sets to watch the *Apollo*'s historic flight. Their

<u>excitement</u> kept them glued to their screens. _____

If something went wrong with the space mission, there would have been deep

<u>sadness and frustration</u>. _____

People worried about the dangers of space travel; loss of life would be a

<u>catastrophe</u>. _____

Neil Armstrong <u>came out</u> of the hatch. _____

Neil Armstrong <u>showed</u> the feelings of everyone watching

when he spoke. _____

Express your enthusiasm. Tell about a recent
event that filled you with excitement.

_____

_____

_____

_____

_____

_____

Word History

These English words come from Latin. Read the words in the left column. Then draw a line to match each word to its origin.

explanation	From the Latin word *deservire*, "to serve zealously."
enthusiasm	From the Old French word *desapointier*, "to remove from office or fail to satisfy the hope of."
express	From the Latin roots *dis* plus *astrum*, which means "star or planet." The word used to mean "the evil influence of a star or planet."
disaster	From the Middle English word *discoveren*, "to reveal." This came from the Latin word part *dis* plus *cooperire*, which meant "to remove a cover."
disappointment	From the Old French word *encorage*, which is from the Latin word *cor*, "heart." It meant "to give heart or make bold."
deserve	
discover	From the Greek *enthousiazein*, "to be inspired by a god."
encourage	From the Latin word *explanare*. *Planus* means "clear."

8-Word Questionnaire

Read and complete the sentences to tell about yourself.

I **deserve** an award for _____.

I would like to **discover** a way to

_____.

If I could have any answer given to me, I would like an **explanation** of

_____.

Circle a verb.
I **express** myself best by
talking   writing.

I have a lot of **enthusiasm** for

_____.

My teacher **encourages** us to

_____.

I get very **disappointed** when

_____.

I would most like to **explore**

_____.

Find the Right Word

Read each question.
Circle the best answer.

For what might you need a compass?	exploration	expectation
What do you do with your opinion?	expose	express
Where is there very little rainfall?	deserve	desert
Which feeling is more unpleasant?	discontinue	disappointment
What do you do when you try to help someone be brave?	courage	encourage
Which is a noun?	enthusiastic	enthusiasm
Which is a terrible thing?	disaster	duster
Which is a verb?	discovery	discover
Which means "to go completely under water"?	submerge	emerge
What might you get after a question?	explanation	exploration

Hink Pinks

Complete the riddles with answers
that rhyme. Choose from
the words in the box.

Word Box

disaster	guess
enthusiasm	master
explore	shore
express	spasm

What is a highway with no signs called?

The _____ _____

What do you do when you look around the beach?

_____ the _____

What do you call it when people are so excited
they're twitching?

An _____ _____

What do you call my little brother
when he's making a big mess?

A _____

of _____

There's Courage in Encourage

What big word can you find in **encourage**? Circle it.

encourage

Encourage means "to give courage to, to inspire with confidence."
Courage means "bravery, the ability to face danger or difficulty."

Complete each
sentence with a word
from the box.

Word Box

courage	encourage
courageous	encouragement
discouraging	encouraging

The _____ firefighter went into the burning building.

Tina needed a lot of _____ from her friends
to try out for the school play.

It takes _____ to tell your friends you
disagree with everyone else's opinion.

If you _____ her, my dog will do funny tricks.

Today is the big game. The weather report is _____.

When you're losing a basketball game, it's _____
to hear the announcer shout out the score.

Write about a time you encouraged someone.

_____

_____

Write about a time when you showed courage.

_____

_____

Three's Company, Four's a Crowd

Three of the words in each big square are related in some way. Cross out the word that does not belong.

2
disappointed | discouraged
disheartened | excited

1
energy | excitement
enthusiasm | gloom

3
disaster | tornado
earthquake | lucky

4
discover | explore
fast | voyage

6
reason | answer
mystery | explanation

5
emerge | come out
hide | develop

A Test Is a Test

I've studied and studied,
I deserve a high grade.
So there's no explanation
Why I feel so afraid.

A test is a test,
Nothing more, nothing less.
I know enough to race through it,
Like a locomotive express.

My parents encourage
Me to work hard all year.
They say I can do it.
But I only feel fear.

A test is a test,
Nothing more, nothing less.
Then why do I know
This will be such a mess?

I'll feel disappointment,
I'll let everyone down.
I'll discover I'm stupid,
A silly old clown.

A test is a test,
Nothing more, nothing less.
But now it's all over.
I did well! Success!

Are the following sentences about the poem true or false?
Circle **T** or **F** for the correct answer.

The writer is looking forward to taking the test. T F

The writer's parents have tried to be helpful
and cheer on the writer. T F

The writer's parents think she will fail. T F

The writer has a definite reason for thinking she will fail. T F

The writer doesn't care if she does well or not on the test. T F

The writer is expecting to find out she's really smart
after taking the test. T F

The writer wonders how long it will take her
to answer the questions. T F

The writer is happy with her test results. T F

The writer is expecting to make a mess of things. T F

The writer is trying to convince herself that a test
is not such a big deal. T F

COMPLETE WORKS
OF SHAKESPEARE

Opposites Tic-Tac-Toe

Read each word. Draw a line through the 3 words that are **antonyms**, or opposites, for that word. The line can go across, down, or diagonally.

express

expression	say	loud
repress	withhold	hold back
do	expert	expand

encourage

discourage	courage	discouraging
persuade	dishearten	shorten
badge	badger	deter

enthusiasm

sadness	glee	energy
dullness	dull	perfect
boredom	boring	bore

disaster

bad	catastrophe	hurricane
accident	star	disease
blessing	benefit	good fortune

You Name It!

Each of the items below needs a name.
Circle the right name, and then explain why you chose it.

A bus that goes slowly and won't take you anywhere interesting:
The Exploration Express or The Boredom Bus?

Why? _____

A place on a mountain you have to travel far to get to,
and once you're there, the view is not so good:
Disappointment Point or Point Excitement?

Why? _____

A homework-helper service: Explanations-R-Us or Do-It-Yourself, Inc.?

Why? _____

A candy store for children who behave:
U-Deserve-It Candy or Candy for Complainers?

Why? _____

_____

_____

An adventurous tour guide who is also a scientist:
Dr. Discover or Mr. Mystery?

Why? _____

_____

_____

Put On Your Thinking Cap

Here are some questions to make you think.

How might you use the words **deserve** and **dessert** together in a sentence?

_____

How are a **disaster** and a **disappointment** similar?

_____

In what way do **discover** and **uncover** mean almost the same thing?

_____

What is the difference between the words **explain** and **explanation**?

_____

Are the words **discourage** and **encourage** antonyms or synonyms?

_____

What is the difference between the words **enthusiasm** and **enthusiastic**?

_____

What do an **express train** and **express mail** have in common?

_____

Why might a successful **exploration** lead to a **discovery**?

_____

Why do you suppose the word **emerge** is found in **emergency**?

_____

Word Chains

Complete the chain for each word. In each circle, write a word that is related to the word just before it. An example is done for you.

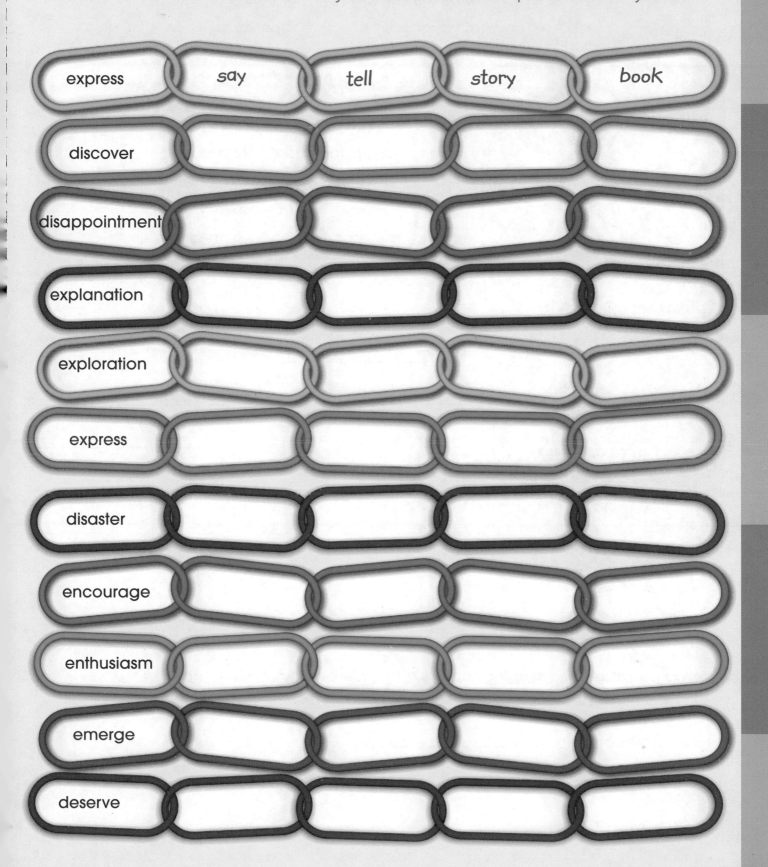

express — say — tell — story — book

discover —

disappointment —

explanation —

exploration —

express —

disaster —

encourage —

enthusiasm —

emerge —

deserve —

One or the Other

Each of the words in the box is either a verb or a noun.
Write each word on a line to show what part of speech it is.

Verbs   **Nouns**

_____   _____

_____   _____

_____   _____

_____   _____

_____   _____

Change these nouns into verbs, for example:

Exploration of shopping malls is a favorite activity of mine. (noun)
I will **explore** every corner of the new mall. (verb)

disappointment _____

explanation _____

discovery _____

Very Short Stories

Write some very short stories using these sentence stems.

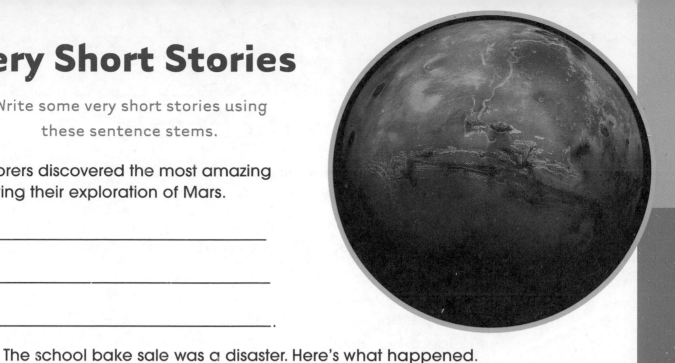

The explorers discovered the most amazing thing during their exploration of Mars.

It was _____

_____

_____ .

The school bake sale was a disaster. Here's what happened.

_____

_____ .

With a little encouragement, Lanie decided to swim in the ocean. But she never thought she'd see

a _____

_____

_____ .

After that, no amount of encouragement could make her get back into the water!

In the year 3000, someone will discover a way

to _____ .

The way it will work is _____

_____

_____ .

Susan opened the mysterious present and, to

her great disappointment, saw _____ .

She immediately _____

_____

_____ .

Joey's explanation for being late to school was the silliest anyone had ever heard. His explanation was that

_____

_____ .

Crossword Puzzle

Use some of the words you learned in Word Group 2 to fill in this puzzle.

Across

1. The car broke down. The bus didn't come. What a
   _____!
2. Our team _____ victorious!
3. A fast train
4. Opposite of success
5. Eager excited feeling
6. Opposite of hide; conceal
7. To make sure you know how to bake a cake, read the directions carefully, or you may be _____.
8. Pleasant

Down

2. Please tell me what happened. I'd like
   an _____.
9. To be worthy of
10. Space _____ took astronauts into the unknown.
11. Inspire someone to try or do better

Word Group 2 Answer Key

32 disaster

33 discover, disappointment, explanation, exploration, express, disaster, encourage, enthusiasm, emerge, deserve

34 explanation, exploration; congregation, injection, description, inspection, confrontation, conversation

35 explain, explanation, explained, exploration, explorer, explore, expressed, expression; exchange, export, exterminate

36 discovery, discovered, discover, discovery, disaster, disappointment

37 1. enthusiasm, 2. express, 3. encourage, 4. disappointment, 5. disaster, 6. deserve, 7. exploration, 8. explanation, 9. discover, 10. emerge

38–39 exploration, discover, enthusiasm, disappointment, disaster, emerged, expressed; answers will vary.

40 deserve, disappoint, disaster, discover, encourage, enthusiasm, explain

41 Answers will vary.

42 exploration, express, desert, disappointment, encourage, enthusiasm, disaster, discover, submerge, explanation

43 Guess Express, Explore the shore, enthusiasm spasm, master of disaster

44 courageous, encouragement, courage, encourage, encouraging, discouraging

45 1. gloom, 2. excited, 3. lucky, 4. fast, 5. hide, 6. mystery

46–47 F, T, F, F, F, T, T, T, T

48 express: repress, withhold, hold back; **encourage:** discourage, dishearten, deter; **enthusiasm:** boredom, boring, bore; **disaster:** blessing, benefit, good fortune

49 The Boredom Bus, Disappointment Point, Explanations-R-Us, U-Deserve-It Candy, Dr. Discover; answers will vary.

50 Answers will vary.

51 Answers will vary.

52 Verbs: express, deserve, encourage, discover, emerge; **Nouns:** exploration, disappointment, enthusiasm, disaster, explanation; disappoint, explain, discover

53 Answers will vary.

54–55 See below.

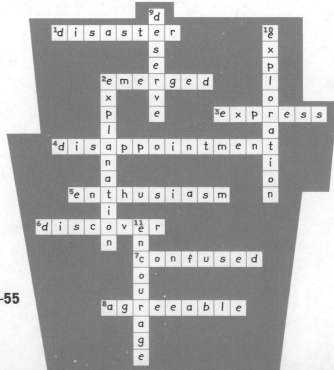

pages 54–55

Dive Into the Dictionary! Definitions tell the meanings of words. When the main entry word is used within the definition, it is printed in **bold** letters.

ex·traor·di·nar·y (ek-**stror**-duh-*ner*-ee) *adjective* Very unusual or remarkable, as in *an extraordinary skill.* ▷ *adverb* **extraordinarily**

ex·treme (ek-**streem**)
1. *adjective* Very great, as in *extreme happiness.* ▷ *adverb* **extremely**
2. *adjective* Farthest. *We reached the extreme edge of the woods.*
3. *noun* One of two ends or opposites, as in *extremes of love and hate.*
4. *adjective* Exciting and very dangerous. *Extreme sports are becoming more popular.*

fas·ci·nate (**fass**-uh-nate) *verb* To attract and hold the attention of. ▷ **fascinating, fascinated** ▷ *noun* **fascination**

for·mal (**for**-muhl) *adjective*
1. Proper and not casual, as in *formal clothes.* ▷ *noun* **formal**
2. Official. *We're waiting for formal permission before we make any plans.* ▷ *adverb* **formally**

for·tu·nate (**for**-chuh-nit) *adjective* Lucky. ▷ *adverb* **fortunately**

fran·tic (**fran**-tik) *adjective* Wildly excited by worry or fear. ▷ *adverb* **frantically**

fre·quent
1. (**free**-kwent) *adjective* Common, or happening often. ▷ *adverb* **frequently**

2. (free-**kwent**) *verb* To visit somewhere often or regularly. ▷ **frequenting, frequented**

fu·ri·ous (**fyu**-ree-uhss) *adjective*
1. Extremely angry. *I was furious when my brother yelled at my best friend.*
2. Fierce or violent, as in *a furious storm.* ▷ *adverb* **furiously**

gen·er·a·tion (*jen*-uh-**ray**-shuhn) *noun*
1. All the people born around the same time, as in *the younger generation.*
2. The average amount of time between the birth of parents and that of their children. A generation is said to be about 30 years.
3. The descendants from a shared ancestor.
4. The process of bringing something into being, as in *the generation of heat by the sun.*

ges·ture (**jess**-chur)
1. *verb* To move your head or hands in order to communicate a feeling or an idea. *The teacher gestured to Nikki that she should sit down.* ▷ **gesturing, gestured** ▷ *noun* **gesture**
2. *noun* An action that shows a feeling. *I sent Maria flowers as a gesture of friendship.*

Use one of the 10 words defined above to finish this joke.

Knock. Knock.
Who's there?
Fran.
Fran who?

_____ to answer the door,
I ran very fast.

Lucky You!

Finish the following sentences.
Choose from the words in the box.
One word is used more than once.

Word Box

Fortuna

fortunate

fortune

fortune cookie

fortune-teller

When you break open a _____ _____,

there is a little slip of paper called a _____ that tells you
a prediction about your future.

I can't see the future. I'm no _____!

At her birthday party, Susan was feeling very _____ that
she had so many good friends.

In Roman mythology, the goddess of fortune

was named _____.

He made a _____ selling cold lemonade on a hot day.

List some things or people you feel fortunate to have in your life.

_____

_____

_____

7-Word Questionnaire

Read each phrase.
Then write your response
on the line.

A time you were **furious**: _____

_____

Something you think is **extraordinary**: _____

_____

Something you are **extremely** interested in: _____

_____

Something that **fascinates** you: _____

_____

Something you are **fortunate** to have: _____

_____

A time you felt **frantic**: _____

_____

A place you like to visit **frequently**: _____

_____

Word Webs

Be a spider and complete each web.

Things you find **fascinating**

Reasons a person might act **frantically**

Things that could be described as **extraordinary**

Things you can express with hand **gestures**

All in the Family

To generate means "to produce or make." Can you guess the connection between **generate** and **generation**? Complete the sentences. Choose from the words in the box. (Some words can be used more than once.)

When people of different ages don't understand each other, the difference is

sometimes described as the _____.

If your parents were born in another country but you were born in the United States,

you are considered a first-_____ American.

Many _____s ago, people did not have electricity in their homes.

The power plant _____s electricity.

Your last name is often passed down from _____ to

_____.

A parent might say to a child, "Your _____ is growing up very

differently than mine did."

A Sticky Situation

Have you ever seen a movie where someone gets stuck in a pool of quicksand? It's an extraordinary situation and fascinating to watch. The mudlike goo quickly sucks the person down, down, with loud, sucking sounds. Frantic, the person grabs hold of something—anything—to try to save himself. If he is fortunate (especially if he is the hero of the movie!), there's a vine hanging conveniently nearby. The person then slowly drags himself to safety. Audiences cheer!

In reality, the danger is never that extreme.

Quicksand is rarely deeper than a few feet, and it won't suck anyone down. Quicksand is just ordinary sand so soaked with water that it can no longer support a person's weight.

What should you do if you find yourself stuck in quicksand on a beach or on the shores of a lake? Don't make big, sudden gestures. That could make you sink lower. Just relax, move slowly, and you'll find yourself floating easily to more solid ground.

Finish these sentences about the passage you just read.
Use words from the box.

Word Box

extraordinary	fascinating	frantic
extremely	fortunately	gestures

In the movies, watching someone struggle in quicksand is so

interesting it is _____ to watch. In movies,

it seems as if quicksand is _____ dangerous.

_____, quicksand is only a few feet deep and not

really dangerous. If you do get stuck in quicksand, however, you're in no

ordinary situation. You're in an _____ one.

To get out of the quicksand, never make _____ movements.

Instead, move slowly, with calm, small _____.

Now write sentences to answer these questions.

What would make a teacher **frantic**?

_____

What invention would be **extraordinary**?

_____

What situation would be **extremely** thrilling?

_____

What would make a person **fascinating**?

_____

What could a friendly **gesture** be?

_____

What makes you feel **fortunate**?

_____

Morning Memo

Complete this memo using words from the box.
Words can be used more than once.

Word Box

extraordinary	frantic
extreme	frequent
formal	furious
fortunate	gesture

April 1
To: All Employees
From: The Boss
Re: Important Information

There have been some very important and _____ events

in our office.

First of all, I am _____ly happy to report that we have

changed our dress code. From now on, women shall wear _____

gowns and men shall wear tuxedos. This will make work feel like a fancy party!

Second, we are very _____ to have a new addition to our staff.

Blip Beep is from Mars and has excellent computer skills. As a welcoming

_____, please stop by her desk to shake her foot. (Don't shake her

hand. Martians consider that rude. Blip Beep would be _____.)

I know everyone has been working very hard. Some of you look a little

_____. Therefore, I suggest you take _____

naps at your desk—at least 5 a day. You can sleep all day if you like.

P.S. If you find this news a little _____, look at the date! April Fools!

Extra! Extra! Extraordinary Events!

Extra- is a prefix that means "above, beyond, more, greater." Just like the word **extra**! Pretend you are a newspaper editor. Write a headline for each event. Use the clue box and the word box for ideas. The first one is done for you.

Clues

Extraterrestrial	**Terrestrial** means "land." **Extraterrestrial** means "from another planet."
Extracurricular	**Curricular** means "relating to classes." **Extracurricular** means "something you do outside of school."
Extraordinary	**Ordinary** means "normal." **Extraordinary** means "very unusual."

Word Box

extreme   fascinate   fortunate   frantic

A girl has memorized every word in the dictionary.

Local Girl Has Extraordinary Vocabulary!

Aliens have landed in the school yard and are running around excitedly.

_____

Many students are joining after-school clubs.

_____

The month of July will be very, very hot, and people who have air-conditioning are very lucky.

_____

The boy who won the Spelling Bee Championship amazed the audience.

_____

Word History

All these words come from Latin! Read the words, and then draw lines to match each word with its origin.

extraordinary	*Forma* means "shape."
extreme	*Fors* means "chance."
fascinate	*Fascinare* means "to cast a spell on."
formal	*Phreneticus* is from *phren*, which means "mind."
fortunate	*Genus* means "birth."
frantic	*Extra* means outside, and *ordinarius* means "order."
frequent	*Extremus* means "out of."
furious	*Frequens* means "numerous."
generation	*Furere* means "to rage."

Crystal Ball

Where will you be in 25 years? Fill in the blanks in each fortune. Choose from the words in the box. When you are finished, close your eyes and put your finger down on the page. Wherever it lands, that is your fortune!

Word Box

extraordinary	fascinate	frantic	generation
extreme	fortunate	frequent	

1. The next _____ in your family will be very large, the largest yet! Also, you will discover something that will _____ the whole world.

2. Even though you will usually be so busy you will feel _____, you will be very _____ to have lots of wonderful things in your life.

3. You will do _____ things: travel the world, learn other languages, and more.

4. You will get to travel abroad _____ly. You will visit _____ climates, like the Arctic and the desert.

Riddle Time

All these riddles have rhyming answers. To complete each answer, write a word from the box.

What do you call an intense nightmare?

An _____ _____

What do you call a fantastic tale? An _____ _____

What do you call a dance you get dressed up for and at which everyone acts ordinary?

A _____ _____

What do you call someone who believes in love and has a lot of energy?

A _____ _____

If you are mad and interested at the same time, you are

_____ and _____.

What do you call a family reunion that includes grandparents, parents, and kids?

A _____ of _____

Word Wizard!

By changing a word's ending, you keep the big idea but change the way the word is used. Nouns can change into verbs, adjectives can change into nouns, and so on.

Word Box

fascinate	furious
fortunate	generation

Pair these **nouns** (naming words) with **adjectives** (describing words). Choose from the words in the box.

Nouns	Adjectives
fortune	_____
fury	_____

Pair this **noun** (naming word) and **verb** (action word). Choose from the words in the box above.

Nouns	Verbs
_____	generate
fascination	_____

Sail Away with Synonyms

These sails have **synonyms** that mean the same or almost the same as a word in the word box. Write each word under or next to the correct boat.

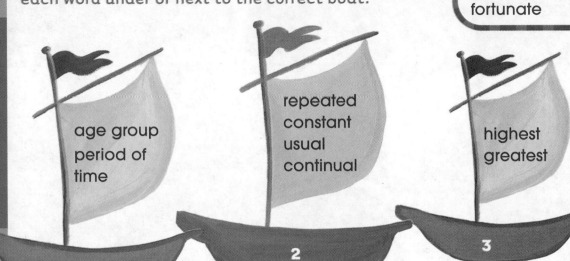

age group
period of time

1

repeated
constant
usual
continual

2

highest
greatest

3

ordered

4

uncommon
exceptional
incredible
amazing

5

frenzied
angry
violent

6

movement
sign
pointing
signal

7

frenzied
wild
raving
raging

8

lucky
victorious
favorable

9

allure, charm
enchant
enthrall
excite
captivate

10

Antonyms

Antonyms are opposites. Each anthill has antonyms for each word in the word box. Write the words on the lines.

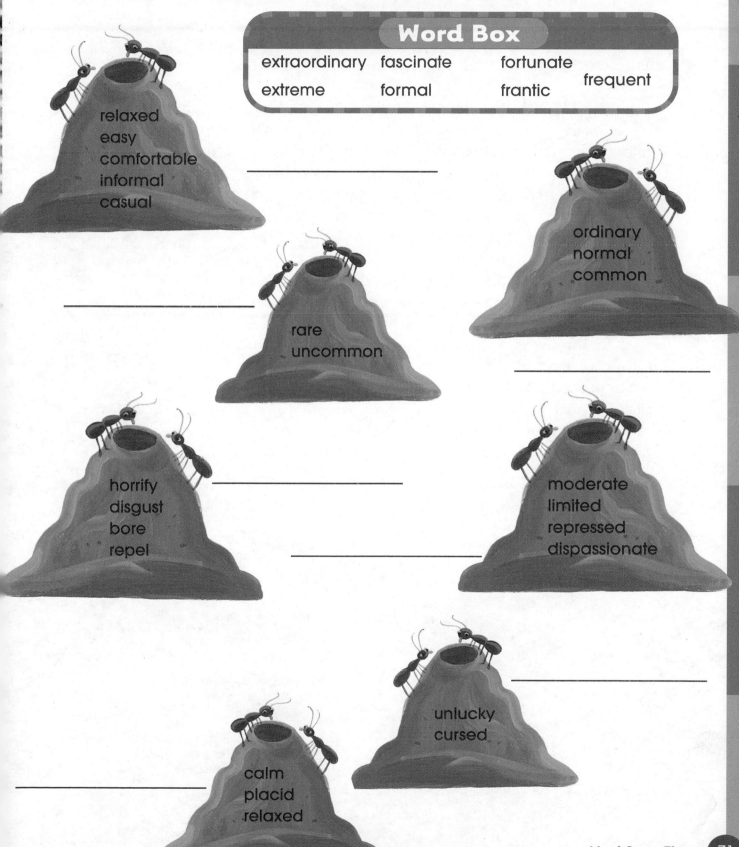

Word Box

extraordinary	fascinate	fortunate
extreme	formal	frantic
		frequent

relaxed
easy
comfortable
informal
casual

_____

rare
uncommon

_____

ordinary
normal
common

_____

horrify
disgust
bore
repel

_____

moderate
limited
repressed
dispassionate

_____

unlucky
cursed

_____

calm
placid
relaxed

_____

Surprise Party

Donna was frantic. She was throwing a surprise anniversary party for her parents and nothing was ready yet. True, this wasn't a formal party. Donna wasn't wearing an expensive, fancy dress or serving an 8-course dinner. Still, she had to put out trays of food, take people's coats, and finish cleaning, all at the same time. It all felt like an extreme amount of pressure.

Lots of friends from her parents' generation were already there. They were talking, joking, and laughing. They were definitely not paying attention to Donna. She kept whispering, "Please be quiet. My parents will be home any minute." But everybody seemed fascinated by everybody else's conversation. Donna was getting frantic, even furious.

"Excuse me, but where is the bathroom?" someone asked. Donna gestured toward a door. These frequent interruptions were making her fall even further behind!

One more person touched her arm. "Yikes!" Donna shouted. "I'm trying to finish everything, so I can surprise my parents."

"Oh, honey," a voice said. "You did surprise us." Donna turned around. Her mom was smiling at her. Her dad reached out and hugged her. By arriving early, Donna's parents had surprised her!

Donna laughed. "Oh, well," she said. "Now you two can help me direct people to the bathroom."

Words can have more than one meaning. Find each word listed below in the story. Then circle the definition that tells how it was used.

Story Word	Definition 1	Definition 2
extreme	farthest	very great
formal	proper, not casual	official
frequent	happening often	to visit a place regularly
furious	extremely angry	fierce or violent
gestured	to move your hands	an action that shows a meaning
generation	the process of bringing something into being	people born around the same time

Now use each word above in a sentence that shows the meaning you didn't circle.

_____

_____

_____

_____

_____

_____

Word Scrambles

Unscramble the words in the right column.
The **synonyms** on the left will give you a clue.
Write the unscrambled words in the boxes where
they best fit. The boxed letters answer
the joke at the bottom of the page.

fancy	oralfm
family	iceratngen
angry	usriofu
busy	ntciraf
special	diyronareaxtr

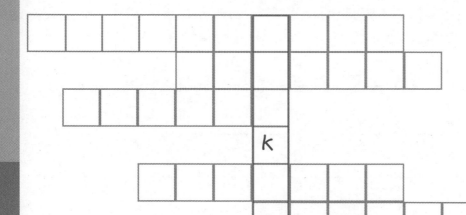

What do you get when you cross a
centipede and a parrot?

A walkie-___ ___ ___ _k_ ___ ___

Bubble Test

Read each question. Then fill in the bubble with the correct answer.

When would you NOT feel **fortunate**?
- ○ You find a quarter
- ○ You get to have a week with no homework
- ○ You miss the bus

What would NOT make you **furious**?
- ○ Being lied to
- ○ Having someone make a big mess in your room and not clean it up
- ○ Winning free tickets to the movies

When would you feel **frantic**?
- ○ Relaxing at home
- ○ Having to buy 20 things at the grocery store and having only 5 minutes before the store closes
- ○ Sleeping peacefully

What does NOT happen **frequently**?
- ○ Trains that leave the station every 15 minutes
- ○ New Year's Eve
- ○ Blinking your eyes

Which idea can you NOT easily express with a hand **gesture**?
- ○ Come here.
- ○ I'm in the bathtub.
- ○ Hello.

Which event is NOT **extraordinary**?
- ○ Winning the Olympics
- ○ Taking out the garbage
- ○ Finding a bag of diamonds

Who Am I?

Read each riddle. Write the answers on the lines. Use the words in the box.

Word Box

extraordinary	frantic
extreme	frequent
fascinate	furious
formal	gesture
fortunate	

I mean "get mad,
to scream and fuss."
I am an adjective.

I'm _____.

You won't find something
like me everyday.
I'm so intense, I'm sometimes scary.
I have 5 syllables.

I'm _____.

"Very, very, very!"
That's what I mean.
I am an adjective.

I am _____.

Chances are you'll use this word
when you see something super-great.
It is a verb; it has 3 syllables.

It is the word to _____.

A wave, a move
with your hands or head,

a _____ can say
what you want to be said.

Lucky you, lucky me,
that from so much we benefit.
A 3-syllable word that means
so much more.

We are very _____.

Hectic, harried,
hassled, do it quick!
The adjective you'd use would be

_____.

To say "usually, common, or very often,"
this 2-syllable adjective is what's meant.

It's _____.

A dress, a dinner, a greeting, not normal.
When something's proper or official,
the word you want to use is

_____.

Sort It Out

Decide whether each word in the box is an **adjective** (describing word) or a **verb** (action word). Then write it in the correct box.

Word Box

extraordinary	fascinate	fortunate	frequent	gesture
extreme	formal	frantic	furious	

Adjectives

_____

_____

_____

_____

_____

_____

Verbs

_____

_____

Chocolate-Chip Cake

Complete this recipe.
Choose from the words in the box.

Word Box

extraordinary	fortunate
extreme	frantic
fascinating	frequent
formal	

Here's an _____ treat to impress your whole family.

You can serve it at a _____ dinner or a party. Who won't

love this combination of chocolate cake and chocolate-chip cookies!

Get out all the ingredients at once. Then you won't become

_____ looking for things while you cook. Follow the

recipe on the box of chocolate-cake mix. Add chocolate chips to the

batter.

Some people find it _____ to watch a cake rise as it

bakes. If your oven has a light, turn it on and watch.

Let the cake cool, and then cover it with chocolate frosting. For

_____ly sweet frosting, sprinkle chocolate chips on the

top! Don't be surprised if your family starts asking for this yummy cake

_____ly! They'll feel very _____ to

have a kid like you around!

Crossword Puzzle

Use the words you learned in Word Group 3 to fill in this puzzle.

Across

1. Out of the ordinary
2. Fast and _____

Down

3. Sending flowers is a nice _____.
4. Opposite of casual
5. My parents belong to an older _____.

Word Puzzle

Unscramble all these words. Then draw a line
to match these words with their **synonyms**.

1. Ticnarf _____   mad

2. tunorfeta _____   wildly excited

3. scinfaatee _____   interest

4. qufenter _____   lucky

5. surfiou _____   often

Now use each of the words you unscrambled in a sentence.

_____

_____

_____

_____

Word Group 3 Answer Key

57 Frantic

58 fortune cookie, fortune, fortune-teller, fortunate, Fortuna, fortune; answers will vary.

59 Answers will vary.

60 Answers will vary.

61 generation gap, generation, generation, generate, generation, generation, generation

62–63 fascinating, extremely, Fortunately, extraordinary, frantic, gestures; answers will vary.

64 extraordinary, extreme, formal, fortunate, gesture, furious, frantic, frequent, extreme

65 Answers will vary.

66 extraordinary/*extra*, extreme/*extremus*, fascinate/*fascinare*, formal/*forma*, fortunate/*fors*, frantic/*phreneticus*, frequent/*frequens*, furious/*furere*, generation/*genus*

67 1. generation, fascinate, 2. frantic, fortunate, 3. extraordinary, 4. frequent, extreme

68 extreme dream, extraordinary story, normal formal, frantic romantic, furious and curious, celebration of generations

69 Adjectives: fortunate, furious; **Noun:** generation; **Verb:** fascinate

70 1. generation, 2. frequent, 3. extreme, 4. formal, 5. extraordinary, 6. frantic, 7. gesture, 8. furious, 9. fortunate, 10. fascinate

71 from left to right: extraordinary, extreme, fascinate, formal, fortunate, frantic, frequent

72–73 very great, not casual, happening often, extremely angry, moved your hands, people born around the same time; answers will vary.

74 See below; talkie

75 You miss the bus, Winning free tickets to the movies, Having to buy 20 things at the grocery store, New Year's Eve, I'm in the bathtub, Taking out the garbage

76 furious, extraordinary, extreme, fascinate, gesture, fortunate, frantic, frequent, formal

77 Verbs: gesture, fascinate; **Adjectives:** formal, frequent, furious, fortunate, frantic, extreme, extraordinary

78 extraordinary, formal, frantic, fascinating, extreme, frequent, fortunate

79 See below.

80 1. frantic/wildly excited, 2. fortunate/lucky, 3. fascinate/interest, 4. frequent/often, 5. furious/mad; answers will vary.

page 79

page 74

Dive Into the Dictionary! Word entries are followed by their pronunciations. The pronunciation guide at the front of the dictionary explains which letters represent which sounds.

glimpse (**glimps**) *verb* To see something very briefly. ▷ **glimpsing, glimpsed** ▷ *noun* **glimpse**

grief (**greef**) *noun* A feeling of great sadness.

hes·i·tate (**hez**-uh-tate) *verb* To pause before you do something. *Zoe hesitated before diving into the freezing-cold water.*
▷ **hesitating, hesitated**
▷ *noun* **hesitation**
▷ *adjective* **hesitant**

im·press (im-**press**) *verb*
1. To make people think highly of you. *Charlie's work impressed his teacher.*
2. To have an effect on someone's mind. *The Statue of Liberty impressed the group.*
▷ *verb* **impresses, impressing, impressed**
▷ *adjective* **impressive**

in·crease (in-**kreess**) *verb* To grow in size or number. ▷ **increasing, increased**
▷ *noun* **increase** (in-**kreess**) ▷ *adverb* **increasingly**

in·de·pend·ent (in-di-**pen**-duhnt)
1. *adjective* Free from the control of other people or things. *The colonists wanted to be independent of England.*
2. *adjective* If someone is **independent,** the person does not want or need much help from other people.

3. independent clause *noun* A sentence that can stand alone and be grammatical, such as the sentence, *"He likes to swim."*
▷ *adverb* **indepentently**

in·gre·di·ent (in-**gree**-dee-uhnt) *noun* One of the items that something is made from, such as an item of food in a recipe.

in·no·cent (**in**-uh-suhnt) *adjective*
1. Not guilty.
2. Not knowing about something. *Tanya was innocent of her aunt's plans.*
▷ *noun* **innocence** ▷ *adverb* **innocently**

in·quire (in-**kwire**) *verb* To ask about someone or something. *Monica inquired about the time of the next commuter train.*
▷ **inquiring, inquired** ▷ *adjective* **inquiring** ▷ *adverb* **inquiringly**

in·spire (in-**spire**) *verb*
1. To fill someone with an emotion, an idea, or an attitude. *Maggie's attitude inspired confidence in her fellow workers.*
2. To influence and encourage someone to do something. *The rock concert inspired me to take guitar lessons.*
▷ *verb* **inspiring, inspired**
▷ *noun* **inspiration** (*in*-spihr-**ay**-shuhn)
▷ *adjective* **inspiring, inspirational** (*in*-spihr-**ay**-shuhn-uhl)

Use one of the 10 words defined above to answer this rhyming riddle.

What do you call a passing sorrow?

Brief _____

What's It Made Of?

Sort all the ingredients from the box.
If an ingredient can go in either circle,
write it in the middle section.

Ingredients for Pizza

Ingredients for a Hamburger

Can you list the ingredients in salad?

_____

_____

_____

Very Short Stories

Write a short story using each story starter.

Tim caught a glimpse of something really cool whizzing by his window.

It was a _____ that _____

_____

_____ .

When Sam heard noises late at night, he hesitated about getting out of bed.

Finally he got up to see what was going on. It was _____

_____ .

Mr. Allen sat down at a restaurant table. He inquired about the special of the day.

The waiter's answer was certainly a surprise. The special of the day was

_____ .

Alison did something very silly. She was trying to impress someone by

_____ , and she _____

_____ !

Oliver baked a crazy cake. Here were the ingredients: _____

_____ _____ _____

"I'm innocent!" the thief cried. "There's been a big mistake! The jewelry was

in my pocket because _____

_____ ."

A Flying Monkey?

Unscramble the words in the right column. The **synonyms**, or words with similar meanings, on the left will give you a clue. Write the unscrambled words in the boxes where they best fit. The boxed letters answer the joke at the bottom of the page.

peek	psimegl
sadness	gfrie
wait	tatesieh
make bigger	creainse
something you add to a recipe	ntinregdie
not guilty	nentiocn
fill with hope	spirein

B
A
B
O
O

What kind of monkey flies to school?

A _____-_____ _____

Vocaburiddles

Read each riddle. Write the answer
to complete it. Choose from
the words in the box.

You're a little nervous, so you wait.

You're doing what's called to _____.

A 1-syllable word that means "a little peek"

_____ is something you can do as you sneak!

When you want someone to think well of you,

_____ them is what you'll try to do.

If you want to say "to make bigger or grow,"

_____ is a verb you'll want to know.

Sadness, sorrow, heartache, woe—

_____ is a feeling that makes us feel low.

All by yourself, on your own—

_____ is an adjective that means "alone."

Eggs and sugar, butter and flour—

with these _____s, you'll have cookies to devour!

When you want an answer to a question,

_____ and you're sure to get one.

Wanted in the Wild West

Help complete this wanted poster to find a thief.
Choose from the words in the box.

Word Box

impress	grief	increase	innocent
inquire	hesitate	independent	glimpse

WANTED

Joe "Bad Guy" McCabe

If anyone catches even a quick

_____ of this man, do not

_____ to call the sheriff.

He has robbed banks and caused people a lot of

_____.

He will try to _____ you with his nice smile and

charm, but do not be fooled. He is NOT _____!

If he _____s about where your money is kept, by

all means do NOT tell him!

Since we can't find him without your help, we have

_____d our reward from $1,000 to $5,000.

Joe "Bad Guy" McCabe does not work with anyone else—he does all

the robberies _____ly.

A Special Recipe

How do you make a decision? You don't need a magic ball to get a glimpse of the future. Just make sure you have these ingredients!

1. Information
Get all the information you can. Talk to people in the know.
And inquire, inquire, inquire!

2. A calm state of mind
Don't rush into making up your mind.
When you're feeling clearheaded, take time to think.

3. An independent view
Don't try to impress anyone. Make a decision based on
what's right for you!

4. Inspiration
Listen to your heart and mind, and be inspired to make
the right choice.

5. Ideas about the future
Imagine the consequence of each action you're considering.

6. Confidence
Feel confident in your decision-making abilities. And once you're
sure about something, don't hesitate. Put your decision into action!

Mix all these
ingredients
together.
Allow to simmer.
Then enjoy your
decision . . .
and your life!

Read the sentences below. Look at the underlined word.
Which part of speech is it? Fill in the bubble beneath the correct answer.

	Noun	Verb	Adjective
You don't need a magic ball to get a <u>glimpse</u> of the future.	○	○	○
Just make sure you have these <u>ingredients</u>!	○	○	○
Once you're sure about something, don't <u>hesitate</u>.	○	○	○
Don't try to <u>impress</u> anyone.	○	○	○
Have your own <u>independent</u> view.	○	○	○
Talk to people in the know and <u>inquire, inquire, inquire</u>!	○	○	○
Listen to your heart and mind, and be <u>inspired</u> to make the right choice.	○	○	○

Write your own recipe for happiness. Use a noun, verb, and adjective in each sentence. Write an **N** above the **nouns**, a **V** above the **verbs**, and an **A** above the **adjectives** you use.

1. _____

2. _____

3. _____

4. _____

Horoscope Helper

Find the dates that include your birthday. Complete your own horoscope first. Then do the others. Use these words: **ingredient**, **innocent**, **inspire**, **inquire**, **hesitate**, **independent**, **impress**, **glimpse**. (Some words are used more than once.)

ARIES (Mar. 21—Apr. 20)

To _____ and

_____ yourself and everyone around you, wear blue tomorrow. This lucky color will make you look great. Good things will happen.

TAURUS (Apr. 21—May 21)

_____ before you ask any

question. Do not _____ about anyone's plans. You might hear something you don't want to hear!

GEMINI (May 22—June 21)

No matter how _____ your pet looks when you get home, he's done something wrong while you were gone.

CANCER (June 22—July 22)

You really like being _____ and never asking for help. But this week it is important to ask for help when you need it.

LEO (July 23—Aug. 22)

Make sure you get at least a quick

_____ at the night sky this week. It will be very pretty.

VIRGO (Aug. 23—Sept. 23)

To _____ your chances of winning a game this week, take off your shoes before you start to play.

LIBRA (Sept. 24—Oct. 23)

If you are going to cook anything this week, make sure you read the list of

_____s very carefully. This is an unlucky week for Libras in the kitchen!

SCORPIO (Oct. 24—Nov. 22)

You will _____ a movie star this week!

SAGITTARIUS (Nov. 23—Dec. 21)

The secret _____ to your success this week is patience.

CAPRICORN (Dec. 22—Jan. 20)

Be careful about trying too hard to

_____ people this week.

AQUARIUS (Jan. 21—Feb. 19)

Your chances of winning the lottery will

_____ this week.

PISCES (Feb. 20—Mar. 20)

Do not _____ to ask questions in class this week.

Pretend you are helping a friend write a movie scene. Rewrite each line of dialogue using more interesting words. Choose from the words in the box.

Say It Out Loud!

Your honor, this man did not commit the crime.

_____

_____

Leave me alone! I'll do it myself!

_____

_____

I demand that you give me more money in my weekly paycheck!

_____

_____

I love her. I want her to think I'm great.

_____

_____

May I ask you a question about where you bought your beautiful hat, ma'am?

_____

_____

You work so hard you make me want to work harder too.

_____

_____

Oh, I don't know what to do. Every time I'm about to do something I think maybe I should change my mind.

_____

_____

_____

Please? Just a quick peek?!

_____

_____

This house is so hard to build. It's giving us all so much trouble.

_____

_____

You have everything you need to be successful—brains, talent, and patience.

_____

_____

Cookbook

Complete this recipe using words from the box.

Here's a recipe sure to _____ your friends.

First, go to the store and get all the _____s.

If you don't see what you want, _____ about

where it is.

When you get home, scoop the ice cream and bananas into

a bowl. Put all the toppings on them. If you love butterscotch,

_____ the amount of topping.

Invite some friends over. Don't _____—

eat the banana split right away, before it melts! It might even

_____you to invent your own sundae and

give it a name!

My inspired sundae is called _____.

Here is what's in it: _____

_____

The Cranky Critic

Pretend you are a movie reviewer!
Complete this review with
the words in the box.

Word Box

glimpse	impress	ingredient
hesitate	increase	inspire

I did not _____ to see the new movie, *Car Chase*,

because the ads made it look very exciting.

They were wrong.

Car Chase did not _____ or _____ me.

This movie doesn't have a single _____ necessary for a good film.

There's no suspense, no good action, no interesting characters. There isn't even a car

chase! And the fact that this movie is three hours long only _____d

my disappointment.

As I walked out, I caught a _____ of the movie playing in the

next theater. *Terror Trucks*: Now *that* looks like a good movie!

Think about a movie or video you've just seen. Write your own review. Use some of the
words from the box to tell what you did or didn't like about it.

_____

_____

_____

_____

Riddle Time

All these riddles have rhyming answers.
To complete each answer, write
words from the box.

Give a pep talk to a group of singers?

_____ the _____

See something you like in a store and ask a question about it?

_____ and _____

What do you call a man who likes to be alone?

An _____ _____

What do you call a robber who is very upset?

A _____ with _____

What is it called when the batter waits uncertainly at home base?

To _____ at the

_____

Wear an outfit meant to wow people!

_____ to _____

Help everyone get along better

_____ the _____

Word History

Read each word history. Write the word from the box that fits.

From the Middle English word *glimpsen*, which means

"to glance." _____

From the Latin word *gravare*, which means "to burden."

The Latin word *gravis* means "heavy." _____

From the Latin word *haesitare*, "to hold fast."

_____

From the Latin word *increscere*, to grow. _____

From the Old French word *dependen*,

"to hang down" _____

From the Latin word *ingredi*, "to enter." (Hint: Think of what enters a bowl in which you're mixing up things

for cookies.) _____

From the Latin prefix **in-**, which means "not," plus the

Latin word *nocere*, "to harm." _____

From the Latin **in-** and *quaerere*, "to seek."

_____

If You Lose a Pet

A pet can be an important part of your family.

A pet can seem like an innocent creature that just wants to love you and be loved. Pets can inspire loving relationships. When they die, it's a great loss.

Your feelings of grief may be very strong. Just seeing a pet's favorite toy may increase your sorrow. These are normal feelings. No one should say, "Oh, it's just a pet. Don't let it bother you."

If you lose a pet, don't hesitate to tell people how you feel. It's a good idea to talk to relatives or friends who have lost a pet, too. They will understand how you feel.

Don't think you have to be independent and handle this all alone. Gather family and friends for a good-bye ceremony. Make a speech, or show some favorite pictures of your animal. Ask everyone to think of something special about your pet and share it. It will make you feel better to remember all the fun you had with your pet and the joy and companionship this animal brought you.

Use words from the box to fill in the blanks.

Hint: You can use a word more than once.

Word Box

grief   hesitate   increase   independent   innocent

The only thing a pet may be guilty of is wanting to love and be loved.

The opposite of **guilty** is _____.

Owning a pet can give you much happiness. Losing a pet brings sorrow.

The opposite of **happiness** is _____.

It's okay to feel needy or rely on others when you've lost a pet.

The opposite of **needy** is _____.

You should quickly confide in people who would understand your feelings.

The opposite of **moving quickly** is _____.

One way to lessen your sorrow is share memories of your pet with others.

The opposite of **lessen** is _____.

Your feelings of well-being may grow with a good-bye ceremony for your pet.

The opposite of the phrase **feelings of well-being** is _____.

What are the qualities you would like in a pet?
List 4 of them here.

1. _____

2. _____

3. _____

4. _____

If you could have any pet in the world, what would it be?

_____

_____

_____

_____

Come On In!

In- is a common prefix. It means "in or not."

Read each sentence, and complete it with an in- word from the box.

Word Box

increase	ingredient	inquire
independent	innocent	inspire

If a query is a question, _____ means "to ask a question."

The puppy's weight has _____d by 5 pounds since it was born.

Two-year-old children are learning to do things themselves.

They want to be more _____.

Things you find in a recipe are called

_____s.

This word literally means "to fill with air." It is used to mean "to fill with emotion, an attitude,

or an idea." _____

In the United States, if a person is accused of a crime,

he or she is _____ until proved guilty.

Democrats, Republicans, and Independents are three political groups in the United States. Why do you suppose Independents are called that?

_____

_____

Synonyms on Vacation

In order to go on vacation, these words need to be packed in the right suitcase, with all their friends. Sort the words in the box into the suitcase that contains its **synonyms**.

glance, flash, peek, brief look

_____

sadness, pain, anguish, trouble

_____

wait
pause

_____

influence
dazzle

_____

grow, expand, enlarge, extend

_____

self-reliant
free

_____

blameless
pure

_____

ask, question, examine

_____

encourage
motivate

_____

Opposites in Order

Draw lines to match the words with their **antonyms**, or opposites.
Then write the words in the first column in **alphabetical order**,
as they would appear in a dictionary.

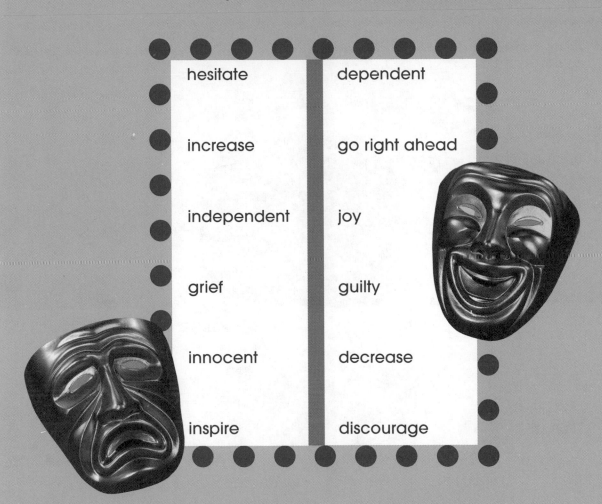

hesitate	dependent
increase	go right ahead
independent	joy
grief	guilty
innocent	decrease
inspire	discourage

Dictionary Order

1. _____   4. _____

2. _____   5. _____

3. _____   6. _____

You Name It!

Each thing described below needs a name. Circle the name that fits each description, and write a short explanation of why you chose that name.

A Hollywood tour company that promises you celebrity sightings:
Glimpse of Greatness or Nothing-to-See Sightseeing?

Why? _____

A train station where the trains never leave on time because the conductors are nervous:
Jumpin' Junction or Hesitation Station?

Why? _____

A new model computer that promises to get you excited about whatever you're working on:
Discourage 3000 or Inspire 3000?

Why? _____

A highway with really great scenery:
Boring Boulevard or The Impress Express?

Why? _____

A grocery store that promises to have everything you need for your recipes:
Ingredient Central or Old Mother Hubbard's?

Why? _____

A new pen for reporters to use:
The Quiet Quill or Inquirers' Ink?

Why? _____

Tic-Tac-Vocab!

Here's a version of tic-tac-toe you can play yourself. Just put an **X** in any square that is true for you. When you are finished, see if you have three in a row.

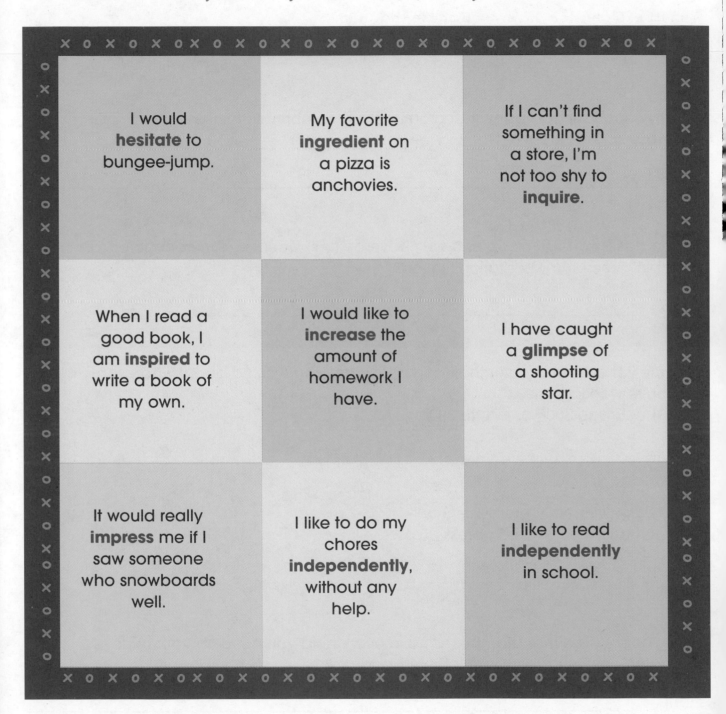

I would **hesitate** to bungee-jump.	My favorite **ingredient** on a pizza is anchovies.	If I can't find something in a store, I'm not too shy to **inquire**.
When I read a good book, I am **inspired** to write a book of my own.	I would like to **increase** the amount of homework I have.	I have caught a **glimpse** of a shooting star.
It would really **impress** me if I saw someone who snowboards well.	I like to do my chores **independently**, without any help.	I like to read **independently** in school.

On another sheet of paper, play tic-tac-spelling with a friend.
Say a vocabulary word out loud (choose from the **bold** words on this page), and have your friend write it in the box of his or her choice. If your friend spells the word correctly, he or she gets to make **X** or **O** in the box.
Take turns spelling words and making **X**'s and **O**'s.

Chef Wanted

Use words from the box to finish this ad.

Chef Wanted

Now hiring for executive-chef position.

Must be able to _____ the other

cooks in the kitchen.

    Must be able to cook dishes that will

    _____ the pickiest customer.

Thorough knowledge of all cooking

_____s (where to find good ones,

how to combine them, and so on).

    Must not be _____ on a

    cookbook.

Must work well both _____ly and

with a team.

    If this sounds like you, do not

    _____ to apply!

_____ within.

Crossword Puzzle

Use the words you learned in Word Groups 3 and 4 to fill in this puzzle.

Across

1. To ask
2. I don't need help. I'm _____.
3. Sadness
4. To add onto
5. He who _____ is lost.
6. Coaches should _____ us play our best.

Down

1. Plead _____ or guilty.
2. A part of something; such as a recipe
7. To _____ the teacher, he did extra credit.
8. Rise up
9. A glance

Word Group 4 Answer Key

82 grief

83 Ingredients for pizza: tomato sauce, pepperoni, crust; ingredients for hamburger: ketchup, mustard, beef patty, bun, lettuce, pickle; ingredients for both: cheese; answers will vary but may include lettuce, cucumber, carrots, peppers, onions, tomatoes

84 Answers will vary.

85 **See below;** hot-air baboon

86 hesitate, glimpse, impress, increase, grief, independent, ingredient, Inquire

87 glimpse, hesitate, grief, impress, innocent, inquire, increase, independent

88–89 noun, noun, verb, verb, adjective, verb, adjective; answers will vary.

90 inspire/impress; Hesitate, inquire; innocent; independent; glimpse; increase; ingredient; glimpse; ingredient; impress; increase; hesitate

91 Answers will vary but should reflect an understanding of the words' meanings.

92 impress, ingredient, inquire, increase, hesitate, inspire; answers will vary.

93 hesitate, impress/inspire, ingredient, increase, glimpse; answers will vary.

94 Inspire the choir, Admire and inquire, independent gent, thief with grief, hesitate at the plate, Dress to impress, Increase the peace

95 glimpse, grief, hesitate, increase, independent, ingredient, innocent, inquire

96–97 innocent, grief, independent, hesitate, increase, grief; answers will vary.

98 inquire, increase, independent, ingredient, inspire, innocent; answers should reflect the idea that the Independent Party is not tied to either of the two major parties.

99 glimpse, grief, hesitate, impress, increase, independent, innocent, inquire, inspire

100 hesitate/go right ahead; increase/decrease; independent/dependent; grief/joy; innocent/guilty; inspire/discourage; dictionary order: grief, hesitate, increase, independent, innocent, inspire

101 Glimpse of Greatness, Hesitation Station, Inspire 3000, The Impress Express, Ingredient Central, Inquirers' Ink; explanations will vary.

102 Answers will vary.

103 inspire, impress, ingredient, dependent, independent, hesitate, Inquire

104–105 **See right.**

pages 104–105

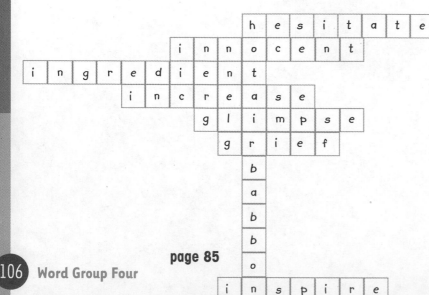

page 85

Dive Into the Dictionary! Syllable breaks are
usually indicated by hyphens (-) or small dots.

in·volve (in-**volv**) *verb* To include something as a necessary part. *The project involves library research.* ▷ **involving, involved** ▷ *noun* **involvement**

launch (**lawnch**)
1. *verb* To put a boat or ship into the water.
2. *verb* To send a rocket up into space.
3. *verb* To start or introduce something new. *The charity launched a campaign to help the homeless.*
4. *noun* A type of boat that is often used for sightseeing ▷ *noun, plural* **launches**
5. **launching pad** or **launch pad** *noun* A place where rockets leave the ground to go up into space.
▷ *verb* **launches, launching, launched**
▷ *noun* **launch**

loy·al (**loi**-uhl) *adjective* Firm in supporting or faithful to one's country, family, friends, or beliefs. ▷ *noun* **loyalty** ▷ *adverb* **loyally**

man·u·fac·ture (man-yuh-**fak**-chur) *verb*
1. To make something, often with machines.
▷ *noun* **manufacturing**, *noun* **manufacturer**
2. To invent something or to make something up. *Eric manufactured an excuse for his lateness.*
▷ *verb* **manufacturing, manufactured**

mas·sive (**mass**-iv) *adjective* Large, heavy, and solid. *Thirty people sat at the massive mahogany table.* ▷ *adverb* **massively**

mi·grate (**mye**-grate) *verb*
1. To move from one country or region to another.

2. When birds **migrate**, they fly away at a particular time of year to live in another region or climate.
▷ *verb* **migrating, migrated** ▷ *noun* **migration** ▷ *adjective* **migratory**

mis·chief (**miss**-chif) *noun* Playful behavior that may cause annoyance or harm to others. ▷ *adjective* **mischievous** (**miss**-chuh-vuhss *or* miss-**chee**-vee-uhss) ▷ *adverb* **mischievously**

mis·sion (**mish**-uhn) *noun*
1. A special job or task. *Our mission is to collect clothing for the flood victims.*
2. A group of people who are sent to do a special job. *My mom and dad are part of the rescue mission.*
3. A church or other place where missionaries live and work.

nav·i·gate (**nav**-uh-gate) *verb*
1. To travel in a ship, an aircraft, or other vehicle using maps, compasses, the stars, etc., to guide you.
2. To sail on or across. *We navigated the river on a rubber raft.*
▷ *verb* **navigating, navigated**
▷ *noun* **navigation, navigator**

neg·lect (ni-**glekt**)
1. *verb* To fail to take care of someone or something. ▷ *adjective* **neglectful**
2. *verb* To fail to do something, especially from carelessness. *She neglected to turn off the iron.*
3. *noun* If a person, building, etc., is suffering from **neglect**, it has not been looked after properly. ▷ *verb* **neglecting, neglected**

Use one of the 10 words defined above to finish the rhyme.

Two boats sailing in the dead of night
couldn't see which way was right.
They almost crashed except for fate.

A shining star helped them _____!

Where Have These Words Been?

Many English words come from Latin. Read the description
of each word, and write the word on the line.
Choose from the words in the box.

Word Box

| involved | manufacture | migrate | mission | neglect |
| loyal | massive | mischief | navigate | |

I come from the Latin word *involvere*, "to enwrap." If you are all wrapped up

in something, you are _____.

I come from the Old French words *leial, loial*. _____

I come from the Latin word *manus* (hand) plus *factus*, "to make." _____

I come from the Old French word *masse* (mass). _____

I come from the Latin word *migrare*, "to change, go, or move." _____

I come from the Old French word *meschever*, "to end badly." _____

I come from the Latin word *missis*, "to send off." _____

I come from the Latin word *navis*, "ship," plus *agere*, "to drive, lead."

_____

I come from the Latin *neg*, "not," and *legere*, "to choose." _____

Synonym Stars

Help these stars shine. Write the **synonym** that fits on each star. Choose from the words in the box.

Word Box

loyal	mission
manufacture	navigate
massive	neglect

Star 1: guide, pilot, maneuver, steer, move
_____ 1

Star 2: goal, purpose, assignment, task, duty
_____ 2

Star 3: forget about, overlook, dismiss, disdain, disregard
_____ 3

Star 4: produce, build, assemble, construct, make
_____ 4

Star 5: large, tremendous, enormous, gigantic, huge
_____ 5

Star 6: reliable, dependable, faithful, devoted, true
_____ 6

Hint: **Synonyms** are words with similar meanings.

Coming in Handy

The Latin word **manus** means "hand." All these words have something to do with hands. Write the words in the correct fingers, according to their meaning. Choose from the words in the box.

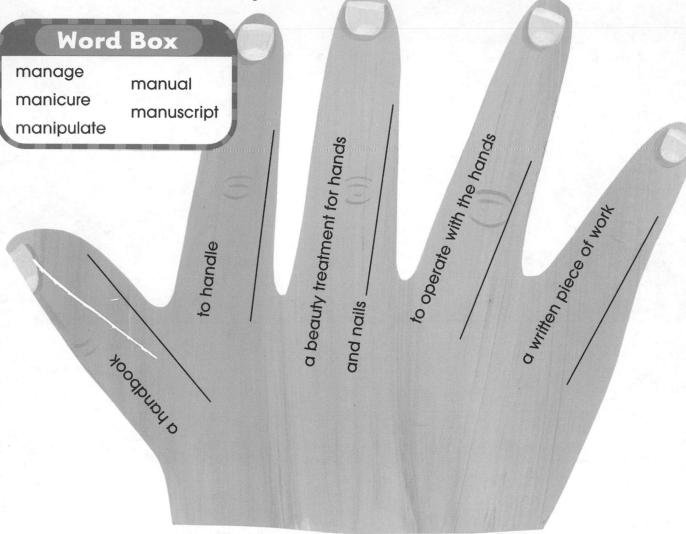

Word Box

manage
manual
manicure
manuscript
manipulate

to handle

a beauty treatment for hands and nails

to operate with the hands

a written piece of work

a handbook

Now complete the sentences using the words in the fingers.

The author gave the final _____ to the publisher.

Jane got a _____ and a massage at the spa.

A string puppet is difficult to operate because there are so many pieces to

_____ at once.

How will I ever _____ baby-sitting five kids at once?

The owner's _____ should tell you how to turn on your computer.

Hink Pinks

Answer these riddles with a rhyme. Choose from the words in the box.

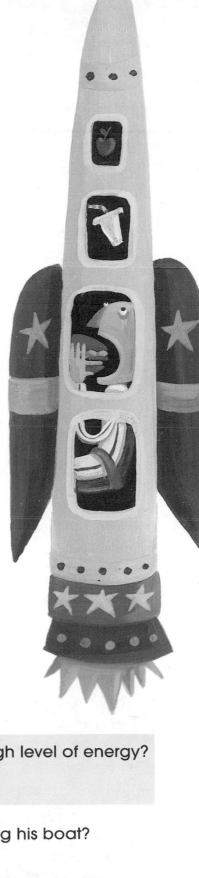

Word Box

ambition	hate	lunch	navigate
architect	involve	migrate	neglect
cliff	launch	mischief	resolve
date	loyal	mission	royal

What meal do astronauts eat as their rocket ship takes off?

A _____ _____

What do you do when you promise to include someone?

_____ to _____ them.

What do you call a queen who always keeps her promises?

A _____ _____

What do you call the time birds fly south?

A _____ to _____

What do you call a rocky edge that's trouble?

_____ _____

What do you call an adventure that requires a plan and a high level of energy?

A _____ with _____

What would you say about a captain who doesn't like steering his boat?

He _____ s to _____ .

What did you do if you didn't pay the man who helped design your house?

_____ the _____

Sisters, Inc.

It was a rainy Saturday afternoon. Jenny felt bored, and so did her little sister Amy. They'd been hanging around doing nothing since breakfast. Their mom had gone upstairs to her office to work long ago. "Don't get into any mischief now," she'd warned the girls on her way out of the kitchen.

"No mischief," Amy sighed. "What are we supposed to do?"

Jenny thought. "We need a mission," she said. "We have to come up with something interesting and important to do."

Amy laughed. "What kind of mission?" she asked. "A mission impossible?"

"No, a mission *possible*," Jenny answered. "Let's launch a business."

"*What?*" Amy asked. Jenny could tell her sister wasn't exactly thrilled by the idea.

"I thought we were sisters," Jenny said, "true-blue, loyal, in-this-together type sisters," she added.

Amy hesitated. "What kind of business?" she asked slowly.

"Well, I haven't thought things through that far," Jenny admitted. "Maybe we could manufacture something."

Both girls looked around the kitchen.

"This doesn't exactly look like a factory," Amy said.

"We do have materials to make something, though," Jenny replied.

"I'm hungry," Amy said.

"That's it!" Jenny snapped her fingers. Then she threw open the cabinets and pulled open the refrigerator door.

"I know something we can make," Jenny told her sister. "Lunch! How much do you think we could charge Mom for delivering a peanut butter and jelly sandwich upstairs!"

Amy grinned, "Sisters, Inc.," she said.

Number the sentences below from **1** to **10** to show the order in which things happened in the story.

_____ Jenny thought they should make lunch.

_____ Jenny thought the girls needed a mission.

_____ Jenny and her sister felt bored.

_____ Jenny wondered what they should charge their mom for delivering a sandwich.

_____ Jenny told Amy sisters should be loyal.

_____ Their mom left the girls and went upstairs to work.

_____ Jenny decided they should start a business.

_____ Jenny hadn't thought about what kind of business to start.

_____ Amy told their mom they wouldn't cause any mischief.

_____ Amy said she was hungry.

Marshmallow Mischief

Use words from the box to complete this newspaper story.

Local Marshmallow _____ Is Miffed!

Max Marsh reported that his marshmallow company was closed yesterday because of _____ in the factory. An entire batch of marshmallow mixture was ruined.

Marsh's factory usually _____s only miniature marshmallows. Some _____ person decided to change that. The troublemaker snuck into the factory and adjusted the machines. Everything started whirring and mixing until one _____ marshmallow popped out. The machines broke. The humongous marshmallow oozed out everywhere. The workers were covered in marshmallow up to their knees. Things were so out of control that Mr. Marsh had to get the police _____d.

"The same thing just happened at the 'S'Mores Store," the police said. "Looks like that fiend Mad Mallow's work. We're on a _____ to track him down."

"I just _____ed this new business," Mr. Marsh said. I really need _____ employees, not pranksters. Who needs one big _____ marshmallow? You'll never fit it in a cup of cocoa!"

Four-Footed Best Friends

Read the paragraph. Complete the sentences
with words from the box.

Word Box

| involved | loyal | massive | mission | neglect |
| launch | loyalty | mischief | navigate | |

People have said that dogs are the most _____

friend a person can ever have. Ask any dog lover and he or she will

_____ into a long explanation of why.

Do you agree? Consider this. A dog is _____ in

every part of your life. It lives in your house, sleeps on your bed, sees you

in good moods and bad moods, and always love you.

For some dogs, like Seeing Eye dogs, _____ is even

more important. These dogs help blind people _____

and find their way around. Seeing Eye dogs' _____ in

life is to help their owners.

If you have a dog, it's important never to

_____ your loyal friend. Remember to

give it food and water every day and to walk and brush

your pet. Pets may get into _____

sometimes, but dogs—whether they are tiny like

Chihuahuas or _____ like the Great

Pyrenees—really are man's best friend.

Space Age

Choose words from the box to complete the sentences. Then use these words in your own sentences.

Word Box

launch	navigate
	navigator
mission	navigation

Imagine it's the year 3000. People are now living on different planets.

They need to get around from planet to planet to shop, visit friends,

or go sightseeing. With this increase in travel, there are space

_____s _____ed every day.

But somebody has to be in charge of all those missions.

Is space _____ the job for you? Could

you _____ your way around the solar system?

Would you like to be a space _____? Write why or

why not, using some of the words from the box. _____

_____

_____

Scrambled Spelling

Unscramble these words and spell them correctly on the lines.
The hints will help you.

robber	feith	_____
sadness	frieg	_____
head of the group	feich	_____
comfort	fliere	_____
short	efbri	_____
accept as true	evliebe	_____
something you add to a mix	diegerntin	_____
get	viceere	_____
harmless trouble	chfeisim	_____

SmartSteer

Choose from the words in the box
to finish the passage.

Word Box

manufactured

massive

migrate

mission

navigate

Have you ever noticed birds just seem to know which direction to fly in in the

winter? If birds can _____ from place to place so easily, why

are people are always getting lost ?

That won't happen to me. I've got SmartSteer on my bike!

SmartSteer is a steering wheel that steers *and* _____s.

All I have to do is hop on my bike. I lean over and speak into my steering

wheel and tell it where I want to go. Then we're off! No matter what my

_____ is—go to the store, wheel over to the playground,

or spin into town—SmartSteer gets me there. It is the coolest thing ever

_____ by a bicycle company.

What would you like to manufacture?
Describe it in three sentences here.

_____

_____

_____

Most Likely to . . .

The suffix **-ive** means "tending to, likely to be."
Read the descriptions, and write the answer,
using the words from the box.

Word Box

argumentative	massive
creative	persuasive
decorative	preservative
expensive	relative
extensive	selective

Likely to keep things fresh. _____

Likely to convince. _____

Likely to be big, have a lot of mass. _____

Likely to go on and on. _____

Likely to start a fight. _____

Likely to make interesting things. _____

Likely to make something more attractive. _____

Likely to be related to. _____

Likely to be choosy. _____

Likely to cost a lot of money. _____

What's My Mission?

A **mission** is a special job or task. Each person, animal, or thing described in the first column has a mission in life. Match the person, animal, or thing to the mission.

congresswoman	to navigate the seas well
birds in the winter	to never neglect the animals in his or her care
pet sitter	to stay involved in his or her child's life
parent	to remain loyal to the people she represents
candy-factory owner	to manufacture great candy
naughty rabbit	to migrate south
dump truck	to make mischief in his burrow
sailor	to get rid of massive amounts of dirt

Now write about one of your missions in life.

_____

_____

_____

Movin' On

immigrant   migrates
immigrate   migrating
immigration   migration
migrant workers   migratory
migrate

Migrate come from a Latin word meaning "to go, change, or move." You'll find this word in many forms. Read the sentences below, and fill in the missing words. Choose from the words in the box.

We studied _____ and learned about people who came to the

United States from other countries.

Many birds _____ south for the winter. Other animals, such as

butterflies, also _____ from one place to another, depending on

the season. The turtle also _____.

There is a forest in California where you can observe the _____ of

ladybugs. They all gather together in one spot to rest!

Some scientists study the _____

patterns of birds.

The United States is a country of

_____s. Everyone who lives here,

except for the Native Americans, came from another

country, or is the descendant of someone who came from another country.

People who go from place to place to work are called _____.

There are many reasons people decide to _____ to the

United States.

If you were an animal capable of _____ once a year, where

would you _____ to? _____

Big Blue

What's blubbery, blue, and the biggest animal in the world? The blue whale. The blue whale is the biggest creature on Earth. It weighs 180,000 pounds. That's nearly 100 tons!

Blue whales eat about 9,000 pounds of food every day—and they don't even have teeth! Instead, the blue whale has long strips of baleen in its mouth. Baleen is made of a substance like your fingernails. This comblike structure hangs from the roof of the blue whale's upper jaw. When the whale opens its massive mouth, seawater filled with plants and tiny fish rushes in. The blue whale then drains the water, using the baleen as a filter to trap food inside its mouth. Gulp!

Like most whales, blue whales feed in cold northern waters. Then they migrate south to have their babies in warmer, more comfortable waters. In fact, the whale baby, called a calf, is born underwater. The mother whale quickly helps her offspring get to the surface for its first breath of air. A baby blue whale may weigh 4,400 pounds, This whale calf can be as long as 2 cars.

There are more than 90 different types of whales. But a mother whale, no matter what type of whale she is, never neglects her baby. She's always on the lookout for danger and keeps her calf close by. The baby whale swims under its mother's flippers. Together they navigate through ocean waters as part of a whale herd, called a pod. The members of a pod are loyal to each other. They stick together for protection and to help provide food for the pod.

Are the following sentences about the passage true or false?
Circle **T** or **F** for the correct answer.

Whales travel through ocean waters in groups called schools.	T	F
Each whale looks out for itself, not caring about others in its group.	T	F
A baby blue whale could be as long two school buses.	T	F
The blue whale has extremely sharp teeth.	T	F
There are more than 90 types of whales.	T	F
Baby whales swim under their mothers' flippers.	T	F
Whales travel to feed in colder waters.	T	F
Whales live in herds called pods.	T	F
Baleen is made out of a substance like human hair.	T	F
Baleen acts like a filter.	T	F

Don't Mis- This!

The prefix **mis-** usually means trouble. It means "bad, badly, or wrong." In fact, everything to which **mis-** attaches itself goes wrong. Use the words **mischief**, **mischievous**, and **mischievously** in the sentences below, and see for yourself!

When left alone, the bear cubs got into all sorts of _____! They knocked over plants, spilled their water, and wrestled playfully with each other. When the zookeeper came in to feed them, they just smiled _____. "Oh, you _____ little creatures!" the zookeeper said.

Now draw a line to match the **mis-** words with their meanings.

misjudge	to pronounce a word incorrectly
misfit	bad luck
misfortune	to get the wrong idea
misprint	to behave badly
misbehave	a mistake in the newspaper
misunderstand	the wrong information
misuse	to use in the wrong way
misinformation	someone who doesn't fit in
mispronounce	understand incorrectly
	to judge wrongly

What's My Name?

Everything below needs a name. Circle the correct, name and then write a sentence explaining why.

An exotic animal shelter that takes in only devoted, dependable animals:
Loyal Lions or Unfaithful Unicorns?

Why? _____

A detective agency that will find the answer to your mystery and also let you go along with them on secret missions:
Solve & !gnore, Inc., or Solve & Involve, Inc.?

Why? _____

A place where birds flying south gather to rest:
Migration Station or The Stay-at-Home Shack?

Why? _____

A motorcycle shop that sells only large bikes:
Massive Motorcycles or Miniature Motorcycles?

Why? _____

A store that sells compasses and maps:
Navigation Central or Get Lost, Inc.?

Why? _____

The slogan for a factory that has made hats since 1920:
Manufacturing Caps Since 1920 or Wearing Caps Since 1920?

Why? _____

The slogan for a travel company that specializes in rocketship tours:
No Mission Too Big! or We'll Never, Ever Launch!

Why? _____

Riddle Rhymes

Finish the riddle rhymes. Choose from the words in the box.

Word Box

loyal	massive	mischief	navigate
manufacture	migrate	mission	neglect

"Tomfoolery, high jinks, shenanigan,"

all mean _____—wipe off that grin!

By your side till the end,

a _____ pal is a true friend.

Cars and clothes, paper and string,

all are _____d things.

A goal, a purpose, a vision, a plan:

a _____'s important for every woman and man.

A giant, a skyscraper, China's Great Wall:

_____ is the word to describe them all.

"Hurry up! Fly straight!"
said the goose to the geese.
"Don't be late! Close your mouth!

This is our chance to _____ south!"

In a ship, in a car, or in a new state,

a map will help you _____.

To describe the time
you didn't pay your dues,

"_____ing your duty" is the phrase to use.

10-Word Questionnaire

Answer these 10 questions to tell about yourself.
Use the highlighted words in your answers.

Which would you rather have, a **massive** block of chocolate or a massive scoop of

ice cream? _____

What are some things in which you are very **involved**? _____

_____

If you were mayor and you could **launch** a new campaign to solve a problem,

what would you do? _____

Is loyalty from your friends important to you? What does it mean to you to have a

loyal friend?_____

If you could run a factory that could **manufacture** anything, what would you

manufacture?_____

If you were a bird, do you think you would enjoy **migrating** south for the winter?

_____

Describe the last time you got into some harmless **mischief**. _____

_____

If you could be part of an exploratory **mission**, where would you want to go?

_____

Are you a good **navigator**? Can you find your way around easily?

_____

What is something that you would never **neglect**? _____

_____

Who's Responsible?

The words in the first column relate in some way to a word in the second column. Draw lines to connect them. Then write sentences using the word pairs.

sailor	navigate
rascal	launch
birds	loyal
astronaut	manufacture
friend	migrate
factory worker	mischief

_____

_____

_____

_____

_____

_____

Dive Into the Dictionary!

The entry words in a dictionary appear in alphabetical order. Words within a given section are also arranged in alphabetical order.

Read For **Facts!** Read For **Fun!**

■SCHOLASTIC

Dive Into the Dictionary!

Dictionary definitions tell the meanings of entry words. A word can have more than one meaning. The most frequently used meaning appears first.

Read For **Facts!** Read For **Fun!**

■SCHOLASTIC

Dive Into the Dictionary!

Entry words in a dictionary are followed by their pronunciation. The pronunciation guide at the front of the dictionary explains which letters represent which sounds.

Read For **Facts!** Read For **Fun!**

■SCHOLASTIC

Dive Into the Dictionary!

In a dictionary, an entry word's syllables (the beats of the word) are usually indicated by small dots or dashes between the syllables. The syllables that should be emphasized are highlighted.

Read For **Facts!** Read For **Fun!**

■SCHOLASTIC

Dive Into the Dictionary!

In a dictionary, an entry word's part of speech—such as noun, verb, adjective, or adverb—appears directly after the entry word. Alternative meanings of the word may have different parts of speech.

Read For **Facts!** Read For **Fun!**

■SCHOLASTIC

SCHOLASTIC
100 VOCABULARY WORDS
KIDS NEED TO KNOW BY **4**th GRADE

SCHOLASTIC
100 VOCABULARY WORDS
KIDS NEED TO KNOW BY **4**th GRADE

SCHOLASTIC
100 VOCABULARY WORDS
KIDS NEED TO KNOW BY **4**th GRADE

SCHOLASTIC
100 VOCABULARY WORDS
KIDS NEED TO KNOW BY **4**th GRADE

SCHOLASTIC
100 VOCABULARY WORDS
KIDS NEED TO KNOW BY **4**th GRADE

Crossword Puzzle

Use the words you learned in Word Groups 4 and 5 to fill in this puzzle.

Across

1. Make or invent
2. Motivate to do better
3. Giant; immense
4. The house looked abandoned and _____.

Down

5. Opposite of "stay put"
6. A raise is a pay _____.
7. _____ minus 10, 9, 8, . . .
8. Find your way

Word Search

Circle these words in the puzzle: **involve**, **loyal**, **migrate**, **mischief**, **mission**. The words can read across, down, and backward. Hint: They may appear more than once.

```
n i o m s s i m a b l p l o m o r c k i n m o s f l i m i s s i o n
b n c p k c r e t l o y a l f g p h w n k j c i a s d l k e w q f o
l v f o a h s h r p l g m a e i v k m i s c h i e f r t y l v x i
m o z d i e r s t o x r t y m o i m n o c d s f p c n o m p l i b s
i l y f h i p c t i m k l b i y t r s l v u t w p a a l y g m r s s
s v n a r e t p a w o k m n o a e b c t r m i g r a t e v c m o p i
c e n p e t a r g i m l o y a l l a y o l x f g h e w r s m p a x m
m r a m i t u y x w m i s s i o n e v l o v n i s e y r o f g b v a
e i n v o l v e w p o r b r e w i y t m x p a k l u f h i m c z o i
t g g r s o p x m v p y r s t a p o m n a c r m o m i s s i o n l a
a l b r a q a d a v o i u s p n a x j l e j k a b t a m c r c o u l
r o r b a t m i t w l o y a l t d o m n v a w r p o c l k e n x f o
g l f h i t e f c v a i y b m n o p x h i g w e r d o f l o x s a e
i s t y o m e o o m n a y p b a b o j a l k o m i s c h i e f m o f
m i s c h i e f i l m o c v m e e m n p o y l d s a s e b g f h o l
```

Word Group 5 Answer Key

107 navigate

108 involved, loyal, manufacture, massive, migrate, mischief, mission, navigate, neglect

109 1. navigate, 2. mission, 3. neglect, 4. manufacture, 5. massive, 6. loyal

110 left to right: manual, manage, manicure, manipulate, manuscript; manuscript, manicure, manipulate, manage, manual

111 launch lunch, Resolve to involve, loyal royal, date to migrate, mischief cliff, mission with ambition, hate to navigate, neglect the architect

112–113 9, 4, 1, 10, 6, 3, 5, 7, 2, 8

114 Manufacturer, mischief, manufacture, mischievous, massive, involve, mission, launch, loyal, massive

115 loyal, launch, involved, loyalty, navigate, mission, neglect, mischief, massive

116 mission, launch, navigation, navigate, navigator; answers will vary.

117 thief, grief, chief, relief, brief, believe, ingredient, receive, mischief

118 migrate, navigate, mission, manufactured; answers will vary.

119 preservative, persuasive, massive, extensive, argumentative, creative, decorative, relative, selective, expensive

120 congresswoman/to remain loyal, birds/to migrate south, pet sitter/to never neglect the animals, parent/to stay involved, candy-factory owner/to manufacture great candy, naughty rabbit/to make mischief in his burrow, dump-truck/to get rid of massive amounts of dirt, sailor/to navigate the seas well

121 immigration, migrate, migrate, migrates, migration, migratory, immigrant, migrant workers, immigrate, migrating, migrate; answers will vary.

122–123 F, F, F, F, T, T, T, T, F, T

124 mischief, mischievously, mischievous; misjudge/to judge wrongly, misfit/someone who doesn't fit in, misfortune/bad luck, misprint/a mistake in the newspaper, misbehave/to behave badly, misunderstand/to get the wrong idea, misuse/to use in the wrong way, misinformation/the wrong information, mispronounce/to pronounce a word incorrectly

125 Loyal Lions, Solve & Involve, Inc., Migration Station, Massive Motorcycles, Navigation Central, Manufacturing Caps Since 1920, No Mission Too Big!; answers will vary.

126 mischief, loyal, manufacture, mission, massive, migrate, navigate, neglect

127 Answers will vary.

128 sailor/navigate, rascal/mischief, birds/migrate, astronaut/launch, friend/loyal, factory worker/manufacture; answers will vary.

129 See answer at right.

130 See below.

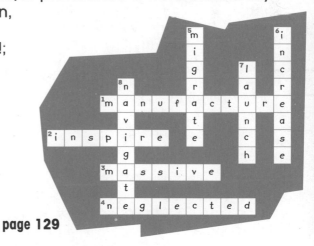

page 129

page 130

Dive Into the Dictionary! The syllables that should
be emphasized, or stressed, when you say a word are highlighted. Here those syllables appear in **bold**.

ob·serve (uhb-**zurv**) *verb*
1. To watch someone or something carefully. *The police have been observing the house.*
2. To notice something by looking or watching. *I observed that Henry had torn his pants.*
3. To make a remark. *Christine observed that the train was late again.*
4. To follow or to obey. *Drivers must observe the speed limit.*
5. To celebrate. *In the United States, people observe Independence Day on July 4th.*
▷ *verb* **observing, observed**
▷ *noun* **observer, observance**

oc·ca·sion (uh-**kay**-zhuhn) *noun*
1. A time when something happens. *Ramón had been to Los Angeles on several occasions.*
2. A special or important event. *Graduation is a happy occasion.*

of·fi·cial (uh-**fish**-uhl)
1. *adjective* If something is **official,** it has been approved by someone in authority. *There will be an official inquiry into the accident.*
▷ *adverb* **officially**
2. *noun* Someone who holds an important position in an organization, as in *a government official.*
3. *noun* In sports, the person who enforces the rules of the game. *The official called a penalty on one of our players.*

o·pin·ion (uh-**pin**-yuhn) *noun*
1. The ideas and beliefs that you have about something. *What's your opinion of our new teacher?*
2. An expert's judgment, as in *a doctor's opinion.*
3. opinion poll A way of finding out what people think about something by questioning a selection of people.

op·por·tu·ni·ty (op-ur-**too**-nuh-tee) *noun*
A chance to do something. *Carla's job gives her the opportunity to travel.* ▷ *noun, plural* **opportunities**

o·rig·i·nal (uh-**rij**-uh-nuhl)
1. *adjective* First, or earliest. *The original cameras were made without lenses.*
▷ *adverb* **originally**
2. *adjective* New, or unusual. *What an original idea!* ▷ *noun* **originality**
3. *noun* A work of art that is not a copy.
▷ *adjective* **original**

per·ma·nent (**pur**-muh-nuhnt) *adjective*
Lasting or meant to last for a long time, as in *a permanent job.* ▷ *noun* **permanence**
▷ *adverb* **permanently**

plunge (**pluhnj**) *verb*
1. To dive into water. *Tom plunged into the pool.*
2. To put or push something in suddenly or with force. *The sergeant showed the new recruits how to plunge their bayonets into the training dummy.*
3. To fall steeply or sharply. *The cliffs plunged to the sea. The temperature plunged.*
4. To do something suddenly, or to make something happen suddenly. *We plunged into action.*
▷ *verb* **plunging, plunged**
▷ *noun* **plunge**

pos·ses·sion (puh-**zesh**-uhn) *noun*
1. Something that you own. ▷ *verb* **possess**
2. If something is *in your possession,* you own it or have it.

pounce (**pounss**) *verb* To jump on something suddenly and grab hold of it. *The lion pounced on its prey.* ▷ **pouncing, pounced**

Use one of the 10 words defined above to answer this riddle.
What happens when a woodpecker delivers a letter offering you a chance of a lifetime?

_____ knocks!

Word History

Most of these words come from Latin. Write the word described on the line. Choose from the words in the box.

Word Box

observe	opinion	permanent
official	original	plunge
		possess

I come from the Latin word *opinare,* "to think." _____

I come from the Latin: *observare, ob-,* means "over," and *servare* means

"to keep watch." _____

I come from the Latin word *officum,* "duty, service." _____

I come from the Latin word *origo,* "source." _____

I come from the Latin word *permanere,* "to remain." _____

I come from the Latin word *plumbicare,*
"to heave something heavy."

_____

I come from the Latin word *possidere.*
Pos- means "master," and *sedere* means

"to sit." _____

Let's Make It Official

Official comes from the Latin word *officum*, meaning "duty or service." Complete the sentences using one of the word endings from the box.

Word Box

-ial	-ially	-iate	-er

A person who enforces the rules at a sports game.

offic_____

A person who holds some sort of authority, such as in the police force or in the army. offic_____

Approved by someone in authority. offic_____

The adverb form of **official**. offic_____

To preside over an official event, such as a marriage. offic_____

If you could make one official rule in your school, what would it be?

_____

_____

_____

The Most Original Origami

Word Box

origin

original

originality

originally

originated

Original comes from the Latin word *origo,* or "source, a place from which things come." It can also mean "new or unusual." Fill in the blanks. Choose from the words in the box.

Our class decided to have an origami contest. The

_____ of origami, the art of paper folding, is

ancient. Origami _____ in Japan.

Each kid in our class got one piece of paper to fold into an

origami shape. We planned to vote on who had the most

_____ piece. Everyone tried to do something

totally new that had never been done before.

_____, the prize was going to be for

_____, but then we decided to give

prizes for creativity and effort, too.

What was the most original thing you ever made?

_____

_____

Patty's Prized Possessions

Possess means "to have." A **possession** is something you have. Which of these two words is a noun? Circle it. Which is a verb? Underline it. Complete the paragraph with words from the box.

Word Box

possess   possessed   possessions   possessive

Patty's room was a mess.

"I have too many _____!" she said. She decided to clean

up. She took everything she _____. She divided her things

into piles.

"This pile will be for all the nicest things I _____," she said.

Patty decided to set up a little museum on her porch. She called her

display Patty's Prized _____. When people came to visit her

museum, they asked if anything was for sale.

"Of course not!" Patty replied. "I'm too _____!"

Rhyming Riddles

Complete the riddles with
words from the box.

Word Box

observe	original
occasion	permanent
official	plunge
opinion	possess
opportunity	pounce

Forever, unchanging,
your own fingerprint:
something that lasts is called

_____.

You have it? You own it?
Well, take a guess.
The verb that you'd use here is

_____.

A party, an event, a happening,
a birthday:

a special _____
doesn't happen every day!

A belief, a sentiment, a personal view:
we may have different

_____s, but I still like you.

Now's your chance, finally, at last!

This _____ is
something you'll want to take fast.

Jump on it fast—quickness counts.
Remember this if you're going to

_____.

A stamp, a signature, a legal seal:
all make something

_____ really for real.

Pay attention, look closely,
not a thing you will miss.

_____ is the verb
that describes all of this.

Dive in! Go ahead!
Don't be scared! Take the leap!

_____ into the
water deep.

Your own good idea, the first,
the real deal:

use the word _____
—a choice that's ideal.

The Wedding Invitation

You are cordially invited to attend the wedding ceremony of Roger Rodent and Mary Mouse. We will exchange wedding vows at this official event. The wedding will take place in the Big Grassy Field (address: 100 Next to the Woods) on the night of the full moon. The ceremony will be performed by the well-known V.I.M. (Very Important Mouse) Judge Longtail.

Our wedding will be a very special occasion. There will be cheese and cheer and the opportunity to see many of our whiskered friends who have moved to the city. We do ask that you observe the following rules so everyone can enjoy the event.

1. Please do not pounce on the cheese trays. Give every mouse a chance to try our wonderful selection of cheeses, from American to Swiss.

2. Please keep all tails out of the wedding aisle, so the bride and groom can scurry with ease.

3. Please do not block the entrance to the nearby mouse hole. An uninvited guest named Kitty may try to attend. A sudden plunge may be required for safety reasons.

Thank you for your consideration. We look forward to sharing this special time with all our family and friends.

Roger Rodent & Mary Mouse

P.S. Instead of presents, please send donations to our favorite charity, the Kitty Alert Fund.

Use words from the box to answer these questions about the story.

Hint: You have to use one word more than once in more than one way.

Word Box

observe	official	plunge
occasion	opportunity	pounce

Roger Rodent and Mary Mouse will exchange wedding vows at an

_____ ceremony.

An _____, Judge Longtail, will perform the ceremony.

The wedding will be an _____ to catch up with old mouse friends.

Roger Rodent and Mary Mouse expect the event to be a very special

_____, complete with snacks.

The mouse bride and groom asked guests to _____ some rules.

In case of an emergency, the bride and groom asked their guests to be ready to

_____ into an open mouse hole.

They've warned their guests not to _____ on the food and that

Kitty may _____ on them.

Suppose Kitty did appear at the wedding ceremony. What would happen next?

Add a new story ending. _____

_____

_____

You Name It

Everything and everyone described below needs a name.
Circle the best name. Then write a sentence explaining your choice.

A policeman who always fills out his paperwork:
Official Officer or Lazy Larry?

Why? _____

A company that caters fabulous parties and important events:
Special Occasions or Stupid Occasions?

Why? _____

A prize-winning newspaper:
The Springfield Observer or *The Springfield Ignorer*?

Why? _____

A playground just for pets:
Pounce & Bounce or Paunch & Brunch?

Why? _____

A company that rents out safes:
Possession Protection or Possession Neglect?

Why? _____

A plumbing company that promises to clear your pipes:
The Perfect Plunge or Clog Company?

Why? _____

Pens with ink that will never erase:
Permanent Pens or Might-Not-Last Markers?

Why? _____

An advertising agency that promises fresh, new ideas:
Original Ideas, Inc., or Old & Boring, Inc.?

Why? _____

Hink Pinks

Answer the riddles with rhyming answers. Choose from the words in the box.

What does a driver do when he notices something in the road and steers out of the way to avoid it?

_____ and _____

What is a place where you can go to get what you want?

_____ _____

What is a mark made with your thumb that won't go away?

a _____ _____

What is it called to own a pretty piece of clothing?

_____ a _____

Write your own riddle linking these word pairs:

announce, pounce _____

_____

lunge, plunge _____

_____

Super-Short Stories

Read the beginnings of these very short stories.
Then complete them using your imagination!

It was a special occasion in the forest, and all the animals were

_____.

As Nan observed the night sky, she saw an amazing thing. She observed that

_____.

The king stood on the castle balcony. He read an official announcement. It said,

"_____."

"Well," said the Sun to the Moon, "If you want my opinion, _____

_____."

Some of his friends thought it was strange, but Joe jumped at the opportunity to

_____.

The museum was very crowded that day because on display were the original

_____!

They were _____.

The genie possessed a special power that allowed him to _____

_____.

When the cat pounced on the mouse, she didn't expect the mouse to say,

"_____."

The Sweetest Job in the World

Word Box

observe	permanent
official	plunge
opinion	possess
opportunity	pounce
original	

It's career day at school, and Dr. Lolly is describing her job as a candy scientist. Help her complete her speech by filling in the missing words. Use the words in the box.

I am a scientist with a special degree in chemistry. I started out working in a company lab. We made new hair dyes. I invented the Outrageous Orange dye I'm wearing right now. But when I heard about the _____ to invent new types of candy, I _____d on the job. I was ready to _____ right in, because I have always had a sweet tooth!

Now I am an _____candy scientist! I studied sugar and invented a way to make it good for people. I think of new kinds of candy that people haven't had before. My ideas have to be very _____. I hold taste-testing sessions. People sample my candy when it's finished and tell me their _____s. I _____ these sessions and write down all the information I hear. The taste tests are an _____ for people to say what they really think about my latest sweet treat.

This is the best job in the world. It's an amazing _____ to please children and adults all over the world and to be creative. I think this will be my job _____ly.

The Missing Link

Each chain is linked by synonyms.
Fill in the missing link in each chain with
a synonym from the box.

Word Box

observe	permanent
occasion	plunge
opinion	possess
opportunity	pounce
original	

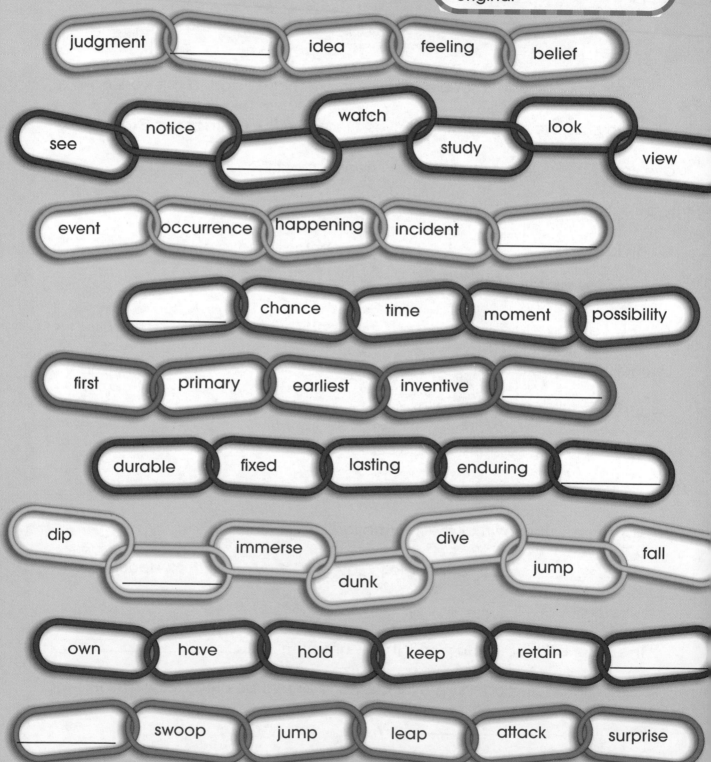

judgment — _____ — idea — feeling — belief

see — notice — watch — _____ — study — look — view

event — occurrence — happening — incident — _____

_____ — chance — time — moment — possibility

first — primary — earliest — inventive — _____

durable — fixed — lasting — enduring — _____

dip — _____ — immerse — dunk — dive — jump — fall

own — have — hold — keep — retain — _____

_____ — swoop — jump — leap — attack — surprise

Who Does What?

Draw a line to connect the noun on the left that would likely be related to each word on the right. Then write sentences using those word pairs.

birdwatcher	opinion
partygoer	plunge
police officer	pounce
film critic	observe
job applicant	occasion
diver	opportunity
cat	official

_____

_____

_____

_____

_____

_____

_____

Renaissance Man

The fourteenth to seventeenth centuries in Europe are called the Renaissance. Renaissance means "rebirth" in French. And this was an era when art and science were reborn.

The Renaissance was a time of great change in Europe. Many people plunged into learning. They explored new ideas and welcomed new experiences.

Renaissance artists created a new way of looking at art. They observed subjects closely, in order to portray them as realistically as possible. In fact, one of art's greatest geniuses worked during the Renaissance. His name is Leonardo da Vinci.

Leonardo was an Italian artist who lived from 1452 to 1519. He possessed amazing artistic skill and an incredible mind. Leonardo drew designs of airplanes, armored tanks, and dozens of other inventions that wouldn't become reality for hundreds of years. But his favorite work—and his most famous—is his portrait of Mona Lisa.

The Mona Lisa is famed for her mysterious smile, as well as for the way light and dark fall on her features. This painting hangs in the Louvre, a museum in Paris, France. But you've seen her face on everything from posters and postcards, to advertisements!

Complete the comparisons below using words from the box.
These comparisons are called **analogies**.

Word Box

observing	permanent
original	possess

Temporary is to _____ as **short lasting** is to **long lasting**.

Looking is to _____ as **hearing** is to **listening**.

_____ is to **first** as **copy** is to **reproduction**.

_____ is to **own** as **donate** is to **give**.

_____ is to **lasting** as **forever** is to **always**.

_____ is to **sightlessness** as **speaking** is to **silence**.

Sell is to _____ as **drop** is to **hold**.

Now make up your own comparison for the word **plunge**.

_____

_____

_____

_____

Grumpy Turtle's Grumpy Day

Finish this entry detailing a day in the life of a grumpy turtle.
Choose from the words in the box.

Word Box

| observing | opinion | original | plunge | pounce |
| occasion | opportunity | permanent | possess | |

March 25

Today I spent a lot of time _____ flies buzzing around my head.

I'm not fast enough to get them. If only I _____ed a flyswatter.

This morning the ducks had a parade. It must have been some sort of special

_____. If you want to know my _____, they

looked very silly quacking and waddling around. They should slow down a little.

However, it was a good _____ for me to listen to their conversation

and hear what's going on in their area of the pond.

I have been thinking a lot about something: I really do not like this yellow spot on

my shell. I wish I could scratch it off, but it seems to be _____.

In the afternoon, I sunned myself on a rock, then _____d into the

water for a long, relaxing soak. I watched a bird _____ on a worm.

They do that all day. They barely eat anything else. Maybe those birds can't think of

anything better to eat. In any case, it's not a very _____ meal.

Alphabetical Order

Without looking at the dictionary pages, put these 20 words in alphabetical order!

massive   _____

possess   _____

neglect   _____

occasion   _____

official   _____

pounce   _____

original   _____

permanent   _____

involve   _____

launch   _____

mission   _____

mischief   _____

observe   _____

opportunity   _____

navigate   _____

plunge   _____

opinion   _____

loyal   _____

manufacture   _____

migrate   _____

Dialogue Doctor

You have been asked to help rewrite the script of the school play! Here are some lines of dialogue from different parts of the script. Use the words in the box to improve each line.

Word Box

observe	opinion	original	plunge	
occasion	opportunity	permanent	possess	pounce

I went to the town square and looked at everyone doing their daily activities.

_____

It's your special day! You can do anything you want! _____

_____

I really need to know what you think. _____

_____

Hurry, go buy the last candy apple before it's gone! _____

_____

Please, just give me a chance! _____

_____

Did you design that dress yourself? I've never seen anything like it! _____

_____

I want to live on the moon forever. _____

_____

I'm ready to jump right into that freezing-cold water. _____

_____

You have an amazing ability to dance! _____

_____

Tic-Tac-Antonym

Look at the word at the top of each puzzle. Then draw a line through the row that contains its **antonyms**. Rows can go up and down, across, or diagonally.

original

old	ancient	perfect
unimaginative	typical	imitation
arise	genial	ridge

observe

remember	chuckle	preserve
ignore	overlook	disregard
serve	reserve	deserve

permanent

temporary	unstable	fleeting
forever	always	lasting
temperment	mood	feeling

official

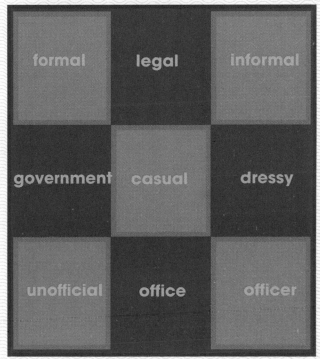

formal	legal	informal
government	casual	dressy
unofficial	office	officer

plunge

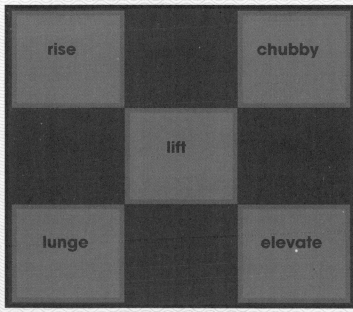

rise		chubby
	lift	
lunge		elevate

10-Sentence Interview

Tell about yourself in 10 sentences! Use the highlighted words in your sentences.

Do you like to **observe** things very closely?

_____

_____

What would you say has been your most **original** creation?

_____

_____

How would you like to spend a special **occasion**, such as your birthday?

_____

_____

Who has made a **permanent** impression on you?

_____

_____

When you grow up, would you like to become an **official**, like the president, a judge, a mayor, or a police officer?

_____

_____

When was the last time you felt as if you were taking a **plunge**?

_____

_____

What is your **opinion** about school uniforms?

_____

_____

What special abilities do you **possess**?

_____

_____

What would you most like the **opportunity** to do?

_____

_____

If you were a cat, do you think you would enjoy **pouncing** on toys or sleeping in the sun?

_____

_____

Firefly Races

Unscramble the words in the right column. The **synonyms** on the left will give you a clue. Write the unscrambled words in the boxes where they best fit. The boxed letters answer the joke at the bottom of the page.

first, new	nallglro
jump	uncepo
event	nooccasi
chance	yoppunitort
have	sesspos
notice	veserob
lasting	trampenen
dive	pelgun
legal	loaffici
belief	noopini

What do fireflies say as they start a race?

_____, _____, _____!

Crossword Puzzle

Use the words you learned in Word Group 6 to fill in this puzzle.

Across

1. Thanks for the _____

2. Celebrate a holiday

3. A birthday is a special _____

4. To own

5. Fresh and new

Down

4. Dive in and take the _____.

6. To swoop down and seize

7. Everyone is entitled to their own _____.

8. Opposite of temporary

9. Referee or umpire

Word Group 6 Answer Key

132 opportunity

133 opinion, observe, official, original, permanent, plunge, possess

134 official, officer, official, officially, officiate; answers will vary.

135 origin, originated, original, Originally, originality; answers will vary.

136 Circle possession. Underline possess, possessions, possessed, possess, Possessions, possessive

137 occasion, opportunity, official, Plunge, permanent, possess, opinion, pounce, Observe, original

138–139 official, official, opportunity, occasion, observe, plunge, pounce, pounce; answers will vary.

140 Official Officer, Special Occasions, *The Springfield Observer,* Pounce & Bounce, Possession Protection, The Perfect Plunge, Permanent Pens, Original Ideas, Inc.; answers will vary.

141 Observe and swerve, Opportunity City, permanent fingerprint, Possess a dress; answers will vary.

142 Answers will vary.

143 opportunity, pounce, plunge, official, original, opinion, observe, opportunity, opportunity, permanent

144 opinion, observe, occasion, opportunity, original, permanent, plunge, possess, pounce

145 birdwatcher/observe, partygoer/occasion, police officer/official, film critic/opinion, job applicant/opportunity, diver/plunge, cat/pounce; answers will vary but should reflect understanding of words' meanings.

146–147 permanent, observing, original, Possess, Permanent, Observing, possess; answers will vary.

148 observing, possess, occasion, opinion, opportunity, permanent, plunged, pounce, original

149 involve, launch, loyal, manufacture, massive, migrate, mischief, mission, navigate, neglect, observe, occasion, official, opinion, opportunity, original, permanent, plunge, possess, pounce

150 Answers should include the following words in order: observed, occasion, opinion, pounce, opportunity, original, permanently, plunge, possess.

151 **original:** unimaginative, typical, imitation; **permanent:** temporary, unstable, fleeting; **plung** rise, lift, elevate; **observe:** ignore, overlook, disregard; **official:** informal, casual, unofficial

152 Answers will vary.

153 **See below;** Ready, set, glow!

154–155 See below.

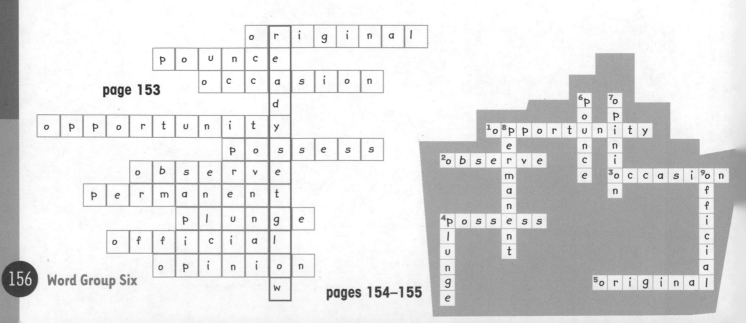

page 153

pages 154–155

Dive Into the Dictionary!

A word can have more than one meaning. The most frequently used meaning appears first.

pres·serve (pri-**zurv**)
1. *verb* To protect something so that it stays in its original state. ▷ *noun* **preserve, preservation** (*prez*-ur-**va**-shuhn)
2. *verb* To treat food so that it does not become spoiled.
3. preserves *noun, plural* Jam. *I love to put apricot preserves on my toast.*
▷ *verb* **preserving, preserved**

pro·ceed
1. (pruh-**seed**) *verb* To move forward or continue. ▷ **preceeding, proceeded**
2. proceeds (**proh**-seedz) *noun, plural* The **proceeds** of an event are the sum of money that it raises. *The proceeds from the book fair went to buy a new encyclopedia.*

pro·duce
1. (pruh-**dooss**) *verb* To make something. *This factory produces cars.*
2. (**prod**-ooss or **proh**-dooss) *noun* Things that are produced or grown for eating, especially fruits and vegetables.
3. (pruh-**dooss**) *verb* To bring something out for people to see. *Nick produced a mouse from his pocket.*
4. (pruh-**dooss**) *verb* To be in charge of putting on a play or making a movie or TV program.
▷ *noun* **producer** ▷ *verb* **producing, produced**

prompt (**prompt**)
1. *adjective* Very quick and without delay. *I received a prompt answer to my question.*
2. *adjective* On time. *Please be prompt for dinner.*
3. *verb* To move someone to action. *The anger in her voice prompted me to drop the discussion.*
4. *verb* To remind actors of their lines when they have forgotten them during a play. ▷ *noun* **prompter**
▷ *verb* **prompting, prompted** ▷ *adjective* **prompter, promptest** ▷ *adverb* **promptly**

pub·lish (**puhb**-lish) *verb* To produce and distribute a book, magazine, newspaper, or any other printed material so that people can buy it.
▷ **publishes, publishing, published**
▷ *noun* **publisher,** *noun* **publishing**

pur·chase (**pur**-chuhss)
1. *verb* To buy something. *My parents purchased a new sofa for the living room.* ▷ **purchasing, purchased** ▷ *noun* **purchaser**

2. *noun* Something that has been bought. *We carried our purchases into the house.*
3. *noun* The act of purchasing. *We saved our money for the purchase of a new stereo.*

quar·rel (**kwor**-uhl)
1. *verb* To argue or to disagree.
2. *noun* An argument.
3. *verb* To find fault. *I can't quarrel with your decision.*
▷ *verb* **quarreling, quarreled**

re·cov·er (ri-**kuhv**-ur) *verb*
1. To get better after an illness or difficulty. *They recovered from the accident.*
2. To get back something that has been lost or stolen. *The police recovered a lot of stolen goods.*
3. To make up for. *In order to recover the time we had lost, we skipped lunch.*
▷ *verb* **recovering, recovered**
▷ *noun* **recovery**

re·flect (ri-**flekt**) *verb*
1. To show an image of something on a shiny surface such as a mirror. *The lake reflected my face.*
2. When rays of light or heat are **reflected,** they bounce off an object. *The diagram shows how a light beam Is reflected when it hits a mirror.*
3. To think carefully. *Bernardo reflected on the meaning of life.*
4. To bring blame or discredit. *His bad behavior reflects on his parents.*
5. To show or to express. *Amanda's clothes reflect her good taste.*
▷ *verb* **reflecting, reflected**
▷ *noun* **reflecting**

re·la·tion (ri-**lay**-shuhn) *noun*
1. A connection between two or more things. *There is a relation between exercise and health.*
2. A member of your family.

Use one of the 10 words defined above to finish this rhyme.

Five men named Smith
attended a celebration.
But they weren't family,
so they had absolutely no

_____.

Personal Histories

In these sentences, each word explains its history. Fill in the word described. Choose from the words in the box.

Word Box

preserve	purchase
proceed	quarrel
produce	recover
prompt	reflect
publish	

I come from the Latin word *procedere*. My roots are *pro* (forward), and *cedere* (to go).

_____

I come from Latin. My roots are *pre* (before) and *servare* (to guard).

_____

I come from the Latin word *promere*, "to bring forth." My roots are *pro* (forth) and *emere* (take, obtain).

_____

I am from the Middle English word *purchasen*, "to try to gain."

_____

I come from the Latin word *recuperare* "to regain, take again."

_____

I come from the Latin word *producere*. My roots are *pre* (forward) and *ducere* (to lead). I mean "to extend, bring forth."

_____

I come from the Latin word *publicare*, "to make public."

_____

I come from the Latin word *queri*, "to complain."

_____

I come from the Latin word *reflectere*. My roots are *re* (again) and *flect* (bend). I used to mean "to throw or bend back." (Hint: Think about what a mirror does with whatever stands before it.)

_____

The Prefix Pre-

Pre- is a prefix you'll see in lots of words. It means "before, in advance." Complete these sentences with words from the box.

We made jam and sealed the jars so it would not spoil.

We had 20 jars of yummy strawberry _____!

The food is _____ in the freezer. It will not spoil.

To _____ photos, put them in an album.

Talking about problems is a good way of _____ the peace.

We visited a wildlife _____ in Kenya, where the animals can't be hunted.

Many people support the _____ of all national parks.

Figure out the meanings of these **pre-** words, and write them on the lines.

prehistoric _____

preheat _____

prejudge (Hint: Think of prejudice.) _____

prepay _____

preshrunk _____

presoak _____

predict _____

precaution _____

prepackaged _____

What a Production!

Complete this job description of a movie producer.
Choose from the words in the box.

Word Box

produce   product
                    productive
producer   production

As a movie _____, I am in charge of making a

movie. I _____ movies. Lots of people work on a

movie: there are a director, actors, writers, costume people, and so on.

Everyone works hard and has a lot to show for it, they are all very

_____.

Want to know how my job got its name? The Latin root *pre-* means

"forward" and *ducere* means "to lead." That's what I do, I lead the

movie forward. I organize the project, hire people, and keep the

_____ on schedule. I have one other really important

job. I make sure there's enough money to pay for everything!

Film _____ is something in which I've been

interested. You can see my finished _____s at your

local movie theater!

If you could be a movie producer, on what sort
of movie would you like to work?

_____

_____

Publish Me!

Word Box

public	publicity	published
publication	publish	publisher

Dear Sir or Madam,

I am writing to you because you are the best _____ in town.

(In fact, you're the only _____ in town!)

I would like you to _____ my book. I've read all the books

you've _____. (Well, there are only two of them.) All your

_____s are great! (Okay, to be honest, the one called *How to Knit*

with Your Mittens On wasn't the most exciting book I'd ever read.) I would love it if my

book could be among them. (As long as it's not on the same shelf as your other

book, *Fun with Cacti*.)

My book is a novel. If I do say so myself, it is fantastic. It has mystery, romance, and

adventure, plus cleaning and cooking tips. I know the reading _____

will just love it, especially the household hints part. Did I mention the main character

also gives instructions on how to repair a car engine while escaping a gorilla who

has stolen a golf cart?

I know my book will sell many copies. I have never had anything

_____ before, so I really want this to work out. I would be happy to

appear on TV and radio shows to talk about my book. If you could provide a gorilla

to go with me, that would be great _____ for your company and

would help you sell even more books!

Look forward to hearing from you.

Sincerely,

Ima Writer

The Winter Street Weekly
Volume 1

A *Note from the Publishers*

Welcome, readers, to the first edition of our street's very first newspaper, brought to you by Kyle and Kisha of 123 Winter Street. We plan to publish this newspaper every week. No purchase is necessary. We will deliver it to your door for free!

We promise to give prompt attention to any and all news about Winter Street. You can help us out. Let us know of any interesting changes or events in relation to Winter Street. If we all keep our eyes and ears open, the news should come pouring in!

Thank you, and keep reading!

Kyle Thomas and Kisha Thomas

Proceed with Caution
by Kyle Thomas

Due to repeated digging by a pesty five-year-old brother, there is a huge hole in one front yard of our street. The address: 123 Winter Street. If you are visiting that home, please watch your step. And feel free to tell that pesty five-year-old to fill in the hole! There is no way he is going to discover pirate treasure in there!

See you next issue.

Look at the underlined words below.
Which part of speech are they? Circle the correct answer.

Kyle and Kisha <u>publish</u> *The Winter Street Weekly.*

      noun   verb   adjective

They pay <u>prompt</u> attention to neighborhood news.

      noun   verb   adjective

In the sentence above, **prompt** means (underline one):

      very quick, without delay   move someone to action.

No one needs to <u>purchase</u> the paper. It is free.

      noun   verb   adjective

They're looking for news in <u>relation</u> to Winter Street.

      noun   verb   adjective

In the sentence above, **relation** means (underline one):

      a connection   a member of the family.

They warn readers to <u>proceed</u> carefully when walking by their home.

      noun   verb   adjective

Again and Again

Re- is a prefix you'll see again and again. It even means "again"! Finish the sentences using one of these **re-** words: **reflect**, **recover**, **relation**.

The surface of the pond _____s the barn.

I have finally _____ed from the chicken pox.

Family members can be called relatives or _____s.

Write the meaning of these **re-** words. Then check your answers in a dictionary.

regain _____

retrace _____

reuse _____

recall _____

rebuild _____

retell _____

redo _____

Mirror, Mirror!

In the Magic Mirror store, each mirror does something different.
Complete the descriptions using words from the box.

Word Box

| reflect | reflection | reflect on |
| reflecting | reflective | reflects |

All of these mirrors _____ your image in a special way.

No matter where you put it, the Murky Mirror always

_____ a gloomy and dark background.

The Massive Mirror is well-known for _____

what you would look like if you were a giant!

The Melody Mirror plays you a song as you

look at your _____.

The Monster Mirror always shows the

_____ of a monster

standing beside you!

The Mood Mirror _____ the mood you're in, even if you

try to hide it! It forces you to _____ what you're

feeling—even if you're not feeling particularly _____.

Family Reunion

Finish these sentences about a family reunion.
Choose from the words in the box.

My whole family got together recently. We had a family reunion. My mother, father,

and brother and I went. My brother and I are so different. He's so weird. How can we

even be _____?

Several of my _____ wore clown suits. They got their invitations

mixed up. They thought they were going to a costume party. More weirdness!

My mom _____ some funny stories about when she and my aunt

were young. They had a juggling act. Neither of them could juggle, so what they really

had was a lot of bumps and bruises.

I talked to a second cousin I had never met before. We have a lot in common. We

both love skateboarding and snowboarding. It was very easy to _____

to him. At least this cousin wasn't weird.

Some younger cousins didn't understand how we were all _____.

They kept asking their mom who everybody was. They couldn't believe she was

anybody's sister or aunt. "But your name's Mom," they kept saying. Little kids are weird, too.

My uncle made an announcement about keeping in touch throughout the year.

He wants to keep up good family _____. Well, they may be weird,

but they are my family!

Write about a relative to whom you relate well. _____

_____

A Day in the Life

Complete this description of the life of an apple. Choose from the words in the box.

Word Box

proceeds	prompt	recover	relations
produce	quarrel	reflection	

It's not easy being an apple. At first things are lovely. I start off in a beautiful

orchard on a tree with all my _____. We have lots of space

between us, so there are rarely any _____s. But when we get

big enough, the farmer _____ to pick us and put us in a

crate. He makes his living selling _____, so he needs to sell us

to a grocery store. Once we are in the crate, the _____ing

begins. "You're bruising me!" "Get your leaf out of my face!" and on and on. But

we're all stuck in the crate. We are _____ly delivered to the

store. Once we are unloaded from the crate, we _____ a little

from the bumpy journey. But here's the best part: At the store, we get polished so

much you can practically see your _____ in our skin! We

look so delicious.

I wonder what's next . . .

Brand Names

Each store, service, or product below needs a name. Circle the better name for each. Then explain why you chose it.

A farm stand that sells only flawless fruits and vegetables:
Perfect Produce or Putrid Produce?

Why? _____

A new kind of freezer bag that promises to keep food fresh for 100 years:
Preserve Packs or Spoil Sacks?

Why? _____

A shop that sells the most accurate mirror anywhere:
Perfection in Reflection or Invisible Images?

Why? _____

A service that delivers pizza in five minutes:
Prompt-O Pizza or Patient Pizza?

Why? _____

_____

Slogan for a daily newspaper: Publishers Since 1919 or Out of Print Since 1919?

Why? _____

A law firm that will help you settle your arguments:
Quiet-the-Quarrels Law Firm or Quarreling Quibblers Law Firm?

Why? _____

A tour company that specializes in family travel:
Relation Vacations or Adventures for Strangers?

Why? _____

A special radar machine finds anything you've lost:
The Recover 3000 or The Stay-Lost 3000?

Why? _____

Hink Pinks

Solve these riddles with phrases that rhyme. Choose from the words in the box.

What do you do when you begin to make bread?

_____ to

_____

What are you doing if you fill a flat bike tire full of air?

_____ the

_____

What do you have to do if you don't turn in your homework?

_____ an

_____

What is a fight with a furry little animal?

_____with a

_____

What are you doing when you think carefully about something and then make a choice?

_____ and _____

What is a place where families can meet to catch a train?

A _____ _____

The Greatest Grocery Store on Earth

Finish this advertisement for a grocery store. Choose from the words in the box.

Word Box

preserves	purchase
proceed	quarrel
produce	recover
prompt	reflect
publish	relation

You won't believe your eyes! Take a moment to _____

on all the reasons you should shop here:

You can _____ top-quality food at low prices. For instance,

this week, peach and apricot _____ are only $1 a jar!

When you first see the _____ aisle, it's hard to

_____ from the shock. It's full of the most colorful, freshest fruits

and vegetables you've ever seen arranged in beautiful pyramids.

Every week in the newspaper, we _____ our special sales so

you know exactly what to look for.

And we have excellent _____ships with our customers. When

you _____ to the checkout line to _____ your

groceries, you'll find that you never have to wait in line. Everyone's happy! Service

is always so _____ people never _____ over

cutting in the line.

It's a great experience. So what are you waiting for? Come on over!

Tic-Tac-You!

You can play tic-tac-toe with yourself! Read the sentence in each square.
Put an **X** in it if it says something true about you. Then look to see
if you have 3 in a row. You can ask a friend to try it after you, using **O**'s.

I love strawberry preserves.	If I could, I would proceed to the front of every line.	My favorite item is bananas.
I am usually prompt arriving at school.	I would like to publish a book someday.	I purchased a book recently.
I saw Siamese fighting fish quarrel.	I like lots of quiet time to reflect on things.	I think it is important that countries have good relations.

The Winter Street Weekly
Volume 2

Quarrel at 123 Winter Street

Soon after our first issue of *The Winter Street Weekly* appeared, an argument broke out at 123 Winter Street. The pesty five-year-old brother did not fill in the hole in the yard. In fact, he dug three more! Parental help was required.

In an effort to keep the peace at 123 Winter Street, all children are now asked to check with parents before doing anything.

Mrs. Thomas Comes Down with Cold

Mrs. Thomas of 123 Winter Street has been sneezing and coughing. We hope she recovers by the weekend so she can take her darling children to the circus.

We would like to use this space to reflect on the good fortune of the Thomas children who live at 123 Winter Street. Their mother is so nice they are sure she could still take them to the circus even if she does have a teeny, tiny, touch of a cold.

A Note from the Publishers

It takes a lot time and care to produce a newspaper of this quality. Soccer practice is starting, and the publishers regretfully announce their time must be spent elsewhere. This is the last issue of *The Winter Street Weekly*.

Kyle Thomas and Kisha Thomas

P.S. If you want some really good news, come watch us play soccer!

Look at the underlined words below. Which part of speech are they? Circle the correct answer.

The major news story was a <u>quarrel</u> over a hole.

noun   verb   adjective

The publishers admit that their parents were needed to <u>preserve</u> the peace.

noun   verb   adjective

The publishers hope their mother <u>recovers</u> quickly from a cold.

noun   verb   adjective

The publishers <u>reflected</u> on their good fortune at having a mom who will take them to the circus, even if she still feels sick.

noun   verb   adjective

In the sentence above, **reflect** means (underline one):

show an image   think carefully.

The publishers won't be able to <u>produce</u> the newspaper anymore because of soccer practice.

noun   verb   adjective

In the sentence above, <u>produce</u> means (underline one):

to be in charge of   to make something   putting on a show

A Floating Elephant?

Unscramble the words in the right column. The **synonyms** on the left will give you a clue. Write the unscrambled words in the boxes where they best fit. The boxed letters answer the joke at the bottom of the page.

you do this with food	spreerev
make into a book	shpubli
go right ahead!	ceedorp
make	crodeup
you need money to do this	sepuchar
fight	relquar
connection	aronelti
quick	poprmt

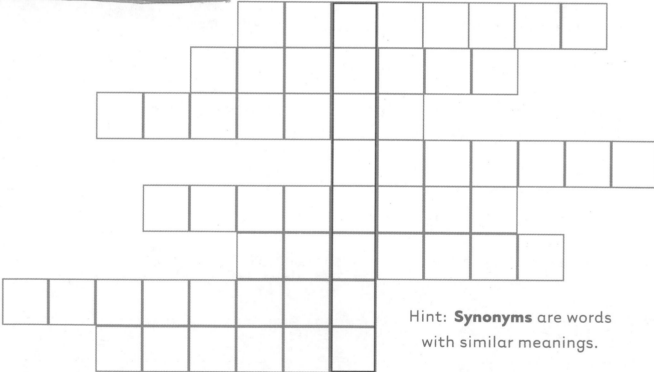

Hint: **Synonyms** are words with similar meanings.

Q. How do you make an elephant float?

A. Some soda, some ice cream, and one large __ __ __ __ __ __ __ !

Pairing Off

Draw lines to connect the words with other words they're likely to be used with in a sentence. Then make up sentences using those pairs.

preserve	shopper
proceed	brother
produce	refrigerator salesperson
prompt	person waiting in line
publish	a cranky child
purchase	factory worker
quarrel	a train
relation	newspaper editor

_____

_____

_____

_____

_____

_____

_____

Look Closely

Read the question.
Then circle the
correct word.

Which is a verb?	purchase	per chance	percent
What does a mirror do?	deflect	replay	reflect
Which involves connection?	elation	relation	elevation
Which means "keeps fresh"?	reserve	preserves	persevere
Which can be unpleasant?	quarrel	barrel	quartz
Which means "to continue"?	produce	procure	proceed
Which is a noun only?	producing	produce	product
Which involves the concept of time?	romp	prompt	prom
Which is a verb?	publish	publication	public

Bubble Test

Read each question. Fill in the bubble next to the correct answer.

Which can you NOT purchase?
- ○ A pie
- ○ A newspaper
- ○ The sun
- ○ A house

What does NOT reflect?
- ○ A mirror
- ○ A deck of cards
- ○ A shiny tabletop
- ○ A still pond

Who is NOT a relative?
- ○ Your mother
- ○ The bird outside your window
- ○ Your brother
- ○ Your cousin

What will NOT preserve something perishable?
- ○ A cooler
- ○ A refrigerator
- ○ A paper bag
- ○ An icebox

What would you NOT be likely to quarrel over?
- ○ Who gets the last piece of gum
- ○ Reading in the library
- ○ Losing a game
- ○ Cutting in line

What would you NOT find in the produce aisle at the supermarket?
- ○ Grapes
- ○ Chocolate
- ○ Carrots
- ○ Onions

What thing does NOT get published?
- ○ A book
- ○ A magazine
- ○ A newspaper
- ○ An orange

Syllable Sort

Draw lines to match the first syllable with the second to make words.
Then use each word in a sentence.

pur	rel
re	flect
pre	chase
quar	ceed
pro	lish
pro	sess
pub	serve
ob	duce
pos	serves

FIRST PLACE WAFFLE MAKER

_____

_____

_____

_____

_____

_____

_____

_____

Crossword Puzzle

Use the words you learned in Word Groups 6 and 7 to fill in this puzzle.

Across

1. Image
2. Fruit or vegetable
3. Opposite of unfaithful
4. Opposite of make up

Down

1. To find, get back
5. A brother or sister, for instance

Word Code

Use this code to figure out the sentences below.
Then fill in the boxes using the words from Word Group 7.

a = b	f = u	j = q	n = m	r = i	v = e
b = y	g = t	k = p	o = l	s = h	w = d
c = x	h = s	l = o	p = k	t = g	x = c
d = w	i = r	m = n	q = j	u = f	y = b
e = v					z = a

[_____] _____ _____ _____!
lfi   hxsllo   tziwvm!

[_____] _____ _____ _____
uiln   gsv   xzpv

_____ _____ [_____] _____
hzov   droo   yv

_____ _____ [_____] _____
fhvw   gl   mvd

_____.
hvvwh.

_____ _____ _____ _____
Wlm'g   ulitvg   gsv   xsvvhvxzpv

_____. _____ _____ _____
izuuov.   Drmmvih'   mznvh   droo

_____ [_____] _____ _____
yv   rm   gsv

_____ _____.
hxsllo   kzkvi

Word Group 7 Answer Key

157 relation

158 proceed, preserve, prompt, purchase, recover, produce, publish, quarrel, reflect

159 preserves, preserved, preserve, preserving, preserve, preservation; answers will vary but should reflect these ideas: before history, heat before, judge before, pay before, shrink before, soak before, tell in advance, be careful ahead of time, packaged before, grade before kindergarten.

160 producer, produce, productive, production, production, product; answers will vary.

161 publisher, publisher, publish, published, publication, public, published, publicity

162–163 verb; adjective; very quick, without delay; verb, noun; a connection; verb

164 reflect, recover, relation; answers will vary but should reflect these ideas: get again, follow again, use again, remember, build again, tell over, do over.

165 reflect, reflects, reflecting, reflection, reflection, reflects, reflect on, reflective

166 related, relatives, related, relate, related, relations; answers will vary.

167 relatives, quarrel, proceeds, produce, quarrel, prompt, recover, reflection

168 Perfect Produce, Preserve Packs, Perfection in Reflection, Prompt-O Pizza, Publishers Since 1919, Quiet-the-Quarrels Law Firm, Relation Vacations, The Recover 3000; answers will vary.

169 Proceed to knead, Preserve the curve, Produce an excuse, Quarrel with a squirrel, Reflect and select, Relation station

170 reflect, purchase, preserves, produce, recover, publish, relation, proceed, purchase, prompt, quarrel

171 Answers will vary.

172–173 noun, verb, verb, verb, think carefully, verb, to make something

174 See below; elephant

175 preserve/refrigerator salesman, proceed/person waiting in line, produce/factory worker, prompt/a train, publish/newspaper editor, purchase/shopper, quarrel/a cranky child, relation/brother; answers will vary but should reflect knowledge of words' meanings.

176 purchase, reflect, relation, preserves, quarrel, proceed, product, prompt, publish

177 The sun, A deck of cards, The bird outside your window, A paper bag, Reading in the library, Chocolate, An orange

178 pur/chase, re/flect, pre/serve *or* serves, quar/rel, pro/ceed *or* duce, pro/duce *or* ceed, pub/lish, ob/serve, pos/sess

179 See below.

180 Preserve our school garden! Proceeds from the cake sale will promptly be used to purchase new seeds. Don't forget the cheesecake raffle. Winners' names will be published in the school paper.

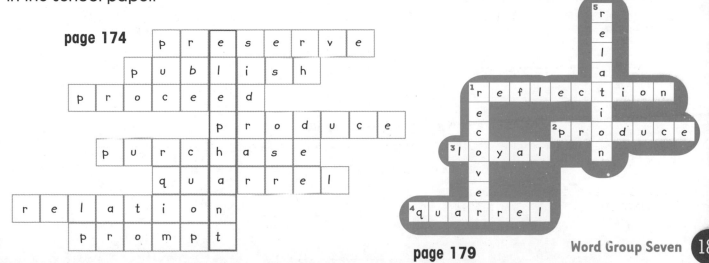

page 174

page 179

Dive Into the Dictionary! Sample sentences appear in *italics* after some of the meanings. These sentences show the word used in context.

re·lease (ri-**leess**) *verb*
1. To free something or someone. *The boy released the trapped squirrel.*
2. If a CD, film, etc., is **released,** it is made available to the public for the first time.
▷ *verb* **releasing, released**
▷ *noun* **release**

rep·re·sent (*rep*-ri-**zent**) *verb*
1. To speak or act for someone else. *My lawyer represented me.*
2. To stand for something. *On a map, water is usually represented by the color blue.*
▷ *verb* **representing, represented**
▷ *noun* **representation**

re·quest (ri-**kwest**)
1. *verb* To ask for something politely. *Visitors are requested to be seated.*
▷ **requesting, requested**
2. *noun* Something that you ask for. *The band played our request.*

re·veal (ri-**veel**) *verb*
1. To make known. *Carmen would not reveal the location of her secret hiding place.*
2. To show or bring into view. *The clouds parted to reveal a beautiful blue sky.*
▷ *verb* **revealing, revealed**
▷ *adjective* **revealing**

sat·is·fy (**sat**-iss-*fye*) *verb*
1. To please someone by doing enough or giving the person enough. *The pizzas soon satisfied the hungry children.*
2. To convince or to free from doubt. *Jackson's alibi satisfied the police.*
▷ *verb* **satisfies, satisfying, satisfied**
▷ *adjective* **satisfied**

scarce (**skairss**) *adjective*
Something that is **scarce** is hard to find because there is so little of it. *Fresh water is scarce on the island.* ▷ *noun* **scarcity**

seize (**seez**) *verb*
1. To grab or take hold of something suddenly. *I seized the rail to keep myself from falling down the steps.*
2. To arrest or capture someone or something. *Police seized the burglars as they came out of the building. The enemy seized the ship.*
▷ *verb* **seizing, seized**

shat·ter (**shat**-ur) *verb*
1. To break into tiny pieces. *The mirror shattered when I dropped it.*
2. To destroy completely or to ruin. *His life was shattered by a tragic car accident.*
▷ *verb* **shattering, shattered**

so·lu·tion (suh-**loo**-shuhn) *noun*
1. The answer to a problem; an explanation.
2. A mixture made up of a substance that has been dissolved in a liquid.

source (**sorss**) *noun*
1. The place, person, or thing from which something comes, as in *the source of the problem.*
2. The place where a stream or river starts.
3. Someone or something that provides information. *An encyclopedia is a useful reference source.*

Use two of the 10 words defined
above to fill in the blanks.

A magician may lose his wand,
and forget if a card is a 9 or a 6.
But one thing a magican will never do

is _____ the

_____ to his tricks.

The Latin Language

All these words come from Latin!
Write the word described on the line.
Choose from the words in the box.

Word Box

release	scarce
represent	seize
request	solution
reveal	source
satisfy	

I come from the Latin verb *relaxare*,

"to loosen." _____

I come from the Latin verb *repraesentare*,
"to bring about immediately, make

present." _____

I come from the Latin verb *requaerere*,

"to see or ask for." _____

I come from the Latin verb *revelare*,

"to unveil." _____

I come from the Latin verb *satisfacere*,

"to do enough." _____

I come from the Latin word *excarpsus*,

"plucked out." _____

I come from the Latin verb *solvere*,
"to loosen or dissolve."

_____

I come from the Latin verb *sacire*,
"to take as one's own, lay claim to."

_____

I come from the Latin verb *surgere*,
"to spring up or spring forth."

_____

Synonym Slots

Each party gift is filled with **synonyms**, words with similar meanings to the words in the box. Write the synonym on the line above each box.

_____

make known
show
display
tell
announce
proclaim
divulge

_____

gratify
appease
pacify
please
content

break
smash
split
crack
damage
destroy

_____

clutch
grab
take

_____

origin
supplier
reference

_____

let go
free
loose
liberate

_____

stand for
symbolize
exemplify
portray
depict

_____

rare
deficient
insufficient
uncommon

Opposites

Draw lines to connect the words with their **antonyms**, or opposites.

seize	disappoint
satisfy	hide, conceal
reveal	let go of, release
scarce	seize, bind, fasten
release	common

Now put a check mark next to the sentence in each pair that makes the most sense.

☐ That delicious meal was satisfying.

☐ That disgusting meal was satisfying.

☐ I really wanted the bag of candy, so I seized it.

☐ I really didn't want the bag of candy, so I seized it.

☐ I tried not to reveal my very private secret.

☐ I tried to reveal my very private secret.

☐ Water is scarce in the desert.

☐ Water is scarce at the beach.

Horoscope Helper

Find the dates that include your birthday. Complete your own horoscope first. Then do the others. Use these words: **represent**, **request**, **reveal**, **satisfy**, **scarce**, **seized**, **shattered**, **solution**, **source**. (Some words are used more than once.)

ARIES (Mar. 21–Apr. 20)

The _____ to whatever problem you're having is closer than you think!

TAURUS (Apr. 21–May 21)

_____ing your true opinions is a good idea this week.

GEMINI (May 22–June 21)

If you really want to _____ your appetite, eat a banana every day this week, and you won't be hungry.

CANCER (June 22–July 22)

If you are suddenly _____ by the desire to eat an entire pizza, don't!

LEO (July 23–Aug. 22)

Watch out for _____ glass on the sidewalk.

VIRGO (Aug. 23–Sept. 23)

Your friends will be a great

_____ of pleasure for you this week.

LIBRA (Sept. 24–Oct. 23)

You will see a white cat this week, and she

will _____ good luck.

SCORPIO (Oct. 24–Nov. 22)

It will rain a lot this week. Opportunities to

go outside will be _____. But there will be one hour when you can go outside and play.

SAGITTARIUS (Nov. 23–Dec. 21)

If you have a special _____ for someone in your family, ask this week. The answer will likely be yes!

CAPRICORN (Dec. 22–Jan. 20)

Do not _____ any personal information to strangers this week—or anytime, ever!

AQUARIUS (Jan. 21–Feb. 19)

_____s to math problems will occur to you very quickly and easily this week.

PISCES (Feb. 20–Mar. 20)

Do not try to _____ everyone when they ask you for things. It is impossible!

Pet Show

Every animal in the pet show gets a prize. Read the description of the animal, and complete the name of the award. Choose from the words in the box.

A sweet, furry, affectionate puppy: Greatest _____ of Comfort.

A rabbit that keeps hiding under the table:

Most Likely to Make Himself _____.

Cat that likes to pounce on mice: Best _____ to a Mouse Problem

A talking parrot who likes to gossip:

Most Likely to _____ Your Secrets

A content, fat cat that's full of food and sitting in a patch of sunlight:

Most _____ Smile

A friendly, sweet snake that gives kisses: Most Likely to

_____ Your Ideas About Scary Reptiles

Lion that won't stop roaring loudly:

Most Likely to Be _____
Back into the Wild

A toucan and monkey who are best friends:

Best _____atives
of the Jungle

Time for Tea

uring the American Revolution, some colonists in Boston, Massachusetts, formed a group called the Sons of Liberty. These patriots did not like the way Great Britain ruled their colony. They decided to do something about it. They held a tea party—a most unusual tea party!

On December 16, 1773, the Sons of Liberty disguised themselves as Native Americans so their identities would not be revealed. They stole aboard a British ship in Boston Harbor. The ship was loaded with tea. The Sons of Liberty didn't drink it. They seized the chests of tea and dumped all 342 of them overboard.

Why did they go to all of this trouble over tea? The real trouble wasn't tea; it was taxes!

Great Britain's King George III allowed the East India Tea Company to bring their tea to the colonies free of tax. Meanwhile, the American companies had to pay taxes. This meant that the British company could sell its tea in the American colonies very cheaply, much more cheaply than American merchants could sell theirs. American business owners weren't happy about lost sales and possible business failure.

Many American colonists felt they had paid more than their fair share of taxes over the years. They also weren't represented in the British government. The colonists argued this was taxation without representation. They had had enough. The solution? A tea party!

Thousands of Bostonians watched quietly as the Sons of Liberty boarded the British ship. Their silence was shattered only by the sound

of wood splitting as the disguised men struck the tea chests with their axes. After the patriots had poured out all the tea, they swept the decks clean and made sure nothing else was damaged. Of course you should clean up after a tea party—even one that's brewing a revolution!

release   represent   reveal   seize   shatter   solution

Choose words from the box to help you answer the questions below.
Hint: You have to use one of the words more than once.

This word + the suffix **-ion** will give you this answer.
A famous slogan of the American Revolution was "No

Taxation Without _____!"

        This word + the verb ending **-ed** will give you this answer.
        The Sons of Liberty wore disguises so their identities would

        not be _____.

The word _____ in the passage means
"to grab," but it could also mean "to arrest."

        The American colonists were looking for a

        _____ to their taxation problems.

This word + the verb ending **-ed** will give you this answer.
When the Sons of Liberty attacked the tea chests with axes, they

_____ the silence of the night . . . and the tea chests!

        This word + the verb ending **-ed** will give you this answer.

        The Boston Tea Party _____ a growing desire
        among many colonists for independence.

This word + the verb ending **-d** will give you this answer.

The Boston Tea Party _____ a flood of
support for a movement that grew into the American Revolution.

Hink Pinks

Complete the rhyming riddles. Choose from the words in the box.

What do you call a store that sells old-fashioned toys?

The _____

_____

What do astronauts say about the lack of oxygen in outer space?

The _____'s

_____!

What do you do when you ask for something fabulous?

_____

the _____

What do you do when you take the skin off fruit to see what color the fruit is inside?

_____

and _____

What is the slogan of a store that promises you'll be happy once you purchase something?

_____ and

_____

What do you do when you grab something on a windy day?

_____ in the

_____

What do you call a broken plate?

A _____ed

_____

What do you do when you speak for a man?

_____ the

_____

What do you do when you ask for a quiz?

_____ a

_____

Job News

Choose from the words in the box to finish the ad.

Word Box

release	satisfy
represent	scarce
request	seize
reveal	source

Reporter Wanted

Local newspaper needs a good reporter. You will be working on many stories. Some

will involve tips and secret information. You must develop a trusting relationship with

your _____s, the people you interview. If they tell you something and

they don't want their name used in the article, you cannot _____ it.

You must not _____ your _____s!

Our readers want the latest and most interesting news. They are a difficult crowd to

_____, so we need good journalists. We _____

late-breaking news as it happens. You must _____ every opportunity

to find a good story. As a reporter you will be _____ing the

newspaper to the public so you must always behave professionally. To apply for this

position, we _____ that you send a some examples of your writing.

Good jobs like this are _____, so apply today.

Would you like a job like this? Why or why not?

_____

_____

Needed: A Name

Honkety HONK HONK

Everything here needs a name. Circle the best name, and explain why you chose it.

Where geese are set free from their pens: Geese Release or Keep the Geese?

Why? _____

_____

Store that sells rare furniture: Scarce Chairs or Common Chairs?

Why? _____

Environmental scientists who have found a way to get rid of smog: Pollution Solution or Pollution Preservation?

Why? _____

A TV show that exposes the truth about life on other planets: Conceal the Unreal or Reveal the Unreal?

Why? _____

Slogan for a store: Satisfaction Guaranteed or Definite Disappointment?

Why? _____

A store that promises window protection so glass doesn't break: No-Shatter Shutters or Shutters That Shatter?

Why? _____

The hotel phone guests can use to call in questions: Guest Request Line or Ignore the Guest?

Why? _____

Rhyming Riddles

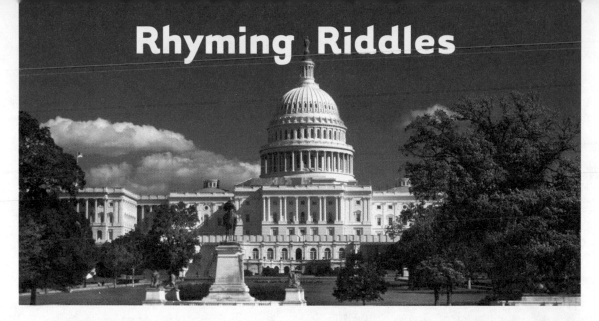

Complete each riddle. Choose from the words in the box.

Got a problem?
An answer's what you need?

A _____ is
what you want, indeed.

If something's been hidden
and then it's shown,

_____ed is the word
that would make that fact known.

A yummy meal, then a delicious pie—
have both; they're sure to

_____!

If you want to say, "Grab! Capture! Take!"

use the word _____,
and there'll be no mistake.

If glass broke into pieces
and all over it scattered,
the window on the ground would be

called _____ed.

The beginning, the origin—
it's a noun, of course.
What you're describing is called a

_____.

Let go; make available; set free—
the verb you'll want to use is

_____.

The congressperson who comes
from the state where you live

is called your _____.

Ask politely; don't be a pest.
A nice way to do this is to

_____.

Word Wizard

Here are some questions to make you think.
Write your answers on the lines.

In what way do you think the words **solve** and **solution** are related?

_____

_____

In what way do you think the words **seize** and **seizure** (a sudden attack or illness or a spasm) are related? Which is a noun, and which is a verb?

_____

_____

In what way do you think the words **reveal** and **revelation** (a very surprising fact that is made known) are related? (Which is a noun, and which is a verb?)

_____

_____

How is **shattering** one's illusions or ideas like shattering glass?

_____

_____

What do you think it means when someone says, "We'd better make ourselves **scarce**"? Why might someone say that?

_____

_____

Why is the Internet considered a **source**?

_____

_____

If you needed a favor from the president, would you use the word **ask** or **request**?

_____

How are the words **satisfy** and **satisfactory** related? (Which is a verb, and which is an adjective?)

_____

_____

Bubble Test

Fill in the bubble next to the correct answer.

Which of the following are
NOT **scarce**?
- ○ Precious, rare diamonds
- ○ Vegetables in Antarctica,
  a continent covered by ice
- ○ People in a big city

Which is NOT a synonym for **solution**?
- ○ Answer
- ○ Problem
- ○ Explanation

What is NOT likely to be **satisfying**?
- ○ A hot bath
- ○ A nap on a bed of rocks
- ○ A good meal

Which is NOT a synonym
for **shattered**?
- ○ Repaired
- ○ Broken
- ○ Splintered

What would you NOT be likely
to **request**?
- ○ A favor
- ○ An ice-cream cone
- ○ An earlier bedtime

Which is NOT a **source** of nutrition?
- ○ An orange
- ○ An avocado
- ○ A rock

Which is an antonym of **seized**?
- ○ Grabbed
- ○ Captured
- ○ Let go

Easy as Pie

This was it. It would be the contest to end all contests. Jack was ready for it: the school pie-eating contest.

Jack had hesitated before he signed up for the contest. He wasn't a very big person. How much could his stomach hold? What would he do when his hunger was satisfied? Could he really represent his class?

His fellow fourth-graders signed a letter requesting that Jack reconsider. They knew how much he liked pie. Jack had to admit it: he *could* eat a lot of pie.

So here he sat, eyeing a long line of pies while everybody eyed him. Blueberry, apple, pear, peach—all those pies looked so yummy. But still they were the source of Jack's nervousness. Suddenly Jack felt like bolting. He wanted to make himself scarce. Jack gazed out at his friends. They gave him the thumbs-up. He knew he had to go through with it.

The whistle blew. Jack seized the first pie. It was apple, his favorite! He took a big bite.

By the time the whistle blew again, Jack had eaten fourteen pieces of pie. The fifth-grader next to him was only on his fourth piece, and he looked a little green.

Jack was clearly the undisputed champ!

All the fourth-graders raced over. They slapped him on the back and gave him high-fives.

"Just wait till next week's town championship!" Jack's friend crowed. "I'll bet you'll eat twenty pieces of pie!"

"Next week?" Jack thought. Twenty pieces? How could he get out of this jam? A solution occurred to him.

"Did I mention I was moving?" he said with a grin.

Here are the word origins for some of the words in the story.
Find the right word, choosing from the ones in the box.

This word probably comes from the Latin word

requaesta, meaning "require." _____

This word probably comes from the Latin word

satis, meaning "enough." _____

This word comes from the Latin word *solutus,*

"to soften or solve." _____

This word comes from the Latin word *surgere,* "to go straight

up or rise," as in the surging of water from where it begins. _____

This word probably comes from the Latin word *excarpsus,* meaning "plucked out,"

as in leaving little behind. _____

This word comes from the Old French word *saisir,* meaning "to put in possession."

_____

This word comes from the Latin word *repraesentare,* meaning "to present."

_____

This word comes from the Latin word *revelare,* meaning "to uncover."

_____

What kind of food-eating contest would satisfy you? _____

_____

Stands for . . .

Each of these signs or symbols **represents** something. Complete the sentence using **represents** and words or phrases from the box. The first has been done for you.

 represents a message for cars to stop.

 _____

 _____

 _____

 _____

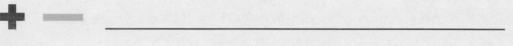 _____

 _____

 _____

 _____

 _____

 _____

Word Sort

Sort the following words into verbs and nouns.
Four of them can be both! Write them in the middle.

Word Box

preserve	quarrel	represent	seize
proceed	recover	request	shatter
produce	reflect	reveal	solution
publish	release	satisfy	source

Nouns   **Verbs**

Now choose 2 words that can be either nouns or verbs. Write 2 sentences for each,
one using the word as a noun and one using it as a verb.

_____

_____

_____

_____

Stop, Thief!

Complete this newspaper article.
Choose from the words in the box.
One word is used more than once.

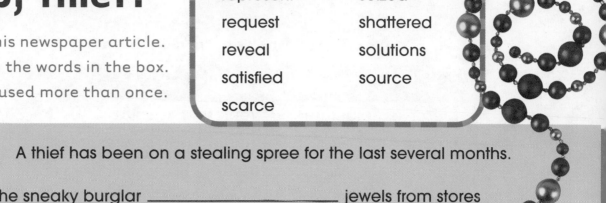

Word Box

represent	seized
request	shattered
reveal	solutions
satisfied	source
scarce	

A thief has been on a stealing spree for the last several months.

The sneaky burglar _____ jewels from stores

and museums across the country.

Police found their first clue when someone reported

_____ glass outside a museum window. The thief

had broken the glass and disabled the alarm system.

A museum _____ said, "We never heard a thing!"

The _____ _____ed that his

name not be revealed. He was embarrassed that the museum's alarm

system was so faulty.

Unfortunately for the thief, he dropped something pretty important

in the museum: his wallet! Even worse, his driver's license was inside. It

_____ed his name and address. The police hurried

over to his apartment. The thief answered the door. Surprise!

The jewel thief's capture _____s a great triumph

for city police. Police Chief Marlowe told the press, "Thank goodness

for that wallet. _____ like this are

_____. We're all very _____.

Super Scrambler

Unscramble the words in the right column. The **synonyms** on the left will give you a clue. Write the unscrambled words in the boxes where they best fit. The boxed letters answer the joke at the bottom of the page.

rare	carces
origin	scoure
show	vealer
set free	leaseer
answer	slountio
ask	quester
broken	edhatters

How did the confused customer request that his eggs be cooked?

May I . . .

Complete all of these requests. Choose from the words in the box.

May I have some of the exotic fruit, even though it is _____?

May I offer a _____ to the problem?

Will you _____ the prisoner? He is innocent.

Will you fix the _____ed plate?

Will you _____ our class in the spelling bee?

May I make one small _____?

May I _____ your secret?

May I quote you as a _____ in my newspaper article?

If you could make one request of our president, what would it be?

_____

_____

_____

The Missing Vowels

All these words are missing their vowels.
Fill in the blanks so the words
are all spelled correctly.

sc ___ rc ___

s ___ l ___ t ___ ___ n

s ___ t ___ sfy

r ___ l ___ ___ s ___

sh ___ tt ___ r

s ___ ___ z ___

r ___ pr ___ s ___ nt

r ___ q ___ ___ st

r ___ v ___ ___ l

s ___ ___ rc ___

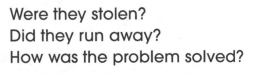

Using at least 4 of the words you completed, write a story about
how the vowels got lost. Some ideas to get you started:

Were they stolen?
Did they run away?
How was the problem solved?

_____

_____

_____

_____

_____

Crossword Puzzle

Use the words you learned in Word Group 8 to fill in this puzzle.

Across

1. The bird was _____ from its cage.
2. When there's not much of something left, it is _____.
3. Break
4. Opposite of question
5. The explorers followed the river to its _____.

Down

1. To stand for or act for
2. _____ him! He's under arrest.
3. To quench or _____ a thirst.
6. Pull back the curtain to _____ the prize.
7. To ask

Word Group 8 Answer Key

182 reveal, solution

183 release, represent, request, reveal, satisfy, scarce, seize, solution, source

184 reveal, satisfy, shatter, seize, source, release, represent, scarce

185 seize/let go of, release; satisfy/disappoint; reveal/hide, conceal; scarce/common; release/seize, bind, fasten; first box in each pair should be checked.

186 solution, Reveal, satisfy, seized, shattered, source, represent, scarce, request, reveal, Solution, satisfy

187 Source, Scarce, Solution, Reveal, Satisfied, Shatter, Released, Represent

188–189 Representation, revealed, seize, solution, shattered, revealed, released

190 Rocking Horse Source, air's scarce, Request the best, Peel and reveal, Buy and Satisfy, seize in the breeze, shattered platter, Represent the gent, Request a test

191 source, reveal, reveal, source, satisfy, release, seize, represent, request, scarce; answers will vary.

192 Geese Release, Scarce Chairs, Pollution Solution, Reveal the Unreal, Satisfaction Guaranteed, No-Shatter Shutters, Guest Request Line; explanations will vary but should reflect knowledge of words' meaning.

193 solution, reveal, satisfy, seize, shatter, source, release, representative, request

194 *reveal* is a verb, and *revelation* is a noun; make ourselves hard to find; request; *solve* is a verb, and *solution* is a noun; you get seized by a seizure, *seize* is a verb, and *seizure* is a noun; shattering illusions is like breaking or destroying them; it's a place where you get information; *satisfy* is a verb, and *satisfactory* is an adjective

195 People in a big city, Problem, A nap on a bed of rocks, Repaired, An earlier bedtime, A rock, Let go

196–197 request, satisfy, solution, source, scarce, seize, represent, reveal; answers will vary.

198 peace, and, addition and subtraction, no or bad, this way, love, musical note, divided by, the United States, yes or good

199 Nouns: solution, source; **Verbs:** proceed, publish, reveal, satisfy, recover, reflect, seize, shatter, release, represent; **Both:** preserve, produce, quarrel, request; answers will vary.

200 seized, shattered, source, source, request, reveal, represent, Solutions, scarce, satisfied

201 See answer at right; scrambled

202 scarce, solution, release, shatter, represent, request, reveal, source; answers will vary.

203 scarce, solution, satisfy, release, shatter, seize, represent, request, reveal, source; answers will vary.

204–205 See answer at right.

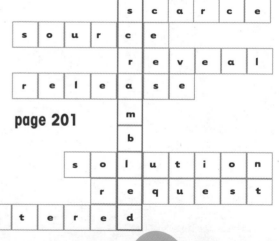

page 201

Dive Into the Dictionary!

Parts of speech, such as noun, verb, adjective, and adverb, are identified in the definition. Alternative meanings can change the part of speech. The different part of speech appears with the other meaning.

stag·ger (**stag**-ur) *verb*
1. To walk or stand unsteadily.
2. If you are **staggered** by something, you are astonished and overwhelmed.
3. When you **stagger** events, you time them so that they do not happen at the same time. *The guards staggered their breaks so that someone was always on duty.* ▷ *adjective* **staggered**
▷ *verb* **staggering, staggered**

sup·port (suh-**port**) *verb*
1. To hold something up in order to keep it from falling.
2. To earn a living for; to provide for. *My mother supports two children.*
3. To help and encourage someone. *We all supported Carmen when she got into trouble.*
▷ *adjective* **supportive**
4. To believe in someone or favor something. *We support environmentalists.*
5. To show to be true. *My findings support your theory.*
▷ *verb* **supporting, supported**
▷ *noun* **support, supporter**

sus·pi·cious (suh-**spish**-uhss) *adjective*
1. If you feel **suspicious,** you think that something is wrong or bad, but you have little or no proof to back up your feelings.
2. If you think that someone seems or looks **suspicious,** you have a feeling that the person has done something wrong and cannot be believed or trusted.

switch (**swich**)
1. *verb* To trade one thing for another. *Let's switch seats.*
2. *verb* To change from one thing to another. *My mom switched from drinking coffee to drinking tea.*
3. *noun* A change or a trade. *There was a switch in the program.*
4. *verb* To turn a piece of electrical equipment on or off. *Switch on the TV.*
5. *noun* A device that interrupts the flow of electricity in a circuit, as in *a light switch.*
6. *noun* A long, thin stick or rod used for whipping.

7. *noun* A quick, jerking motion. *The cow drove the flies away with a switch of its tail.*
8. *noun* A section of railroad track used to move a train from one track to another. ▷ *verb* **switch**
▷ *verb* **switches, switching, switched**
▷ *noun, plural* **switches**

tack·le (**tak**-uhl)
1. *verb* In football, if you **tackle** someone, you knock or throw the person to the ground in order to stop forward progress. ▷ *noun* **tackle, tackler**
2. *verb* To deal with a problem or difficulty. *We must tackle the problem of vandalism.*
3. *noun* The equipment that you need for a particular activity, as in *fishing tackle.*
4. *noun* A system of ropes and pulleys used to raise, lower, or move heavy loads.
▷ *verb* **tackling, tackled**

ter·ri·fy (**ter**-uh-fye) *verb* To frighten greatly; to fill someone with terror. ▷ **terrifies, terrifying, terrified** ▷ *adjective* **terrifying** ▷ *adverb* **terrifyingly**

ter·ri·to·ry (**ter**-uh-tor-ee) *noun*
1. Any large area of land; a region, as in *enemy territory.*
2. The land and waters under the control of a state, nation, or ruler.
3. A part of the United States not admitted as a state.
▷ *noun, plural* **territories**
▷ *adjective* **territorial**

thor·ough (**thur**-oh) *adjective* If you are **thorough,** you do a job carefully and completely. ▷ *noun* **thoroughness**
▷ *adverb* **thoroughly**

threat·en (**thret**-uhn) *verb* If someone or something **threatens** you, it frightens you or puts you in danger. ▷ **threatening, threatened**

tra·di·tion (truh-**dish**-uhn) *noun*
1. The handing down of customs, ideas, and beliefs from one generation to the next.
2. A custom, an idea, or a belief that is handed down in this way.
▷ *adjective* **traditional**

Use one of the 10 words defined above to fill in the blank.

Show your _____ for our clean-environment group. Take a bath!

Words from Around the Globe

Read each word's history. Write the correct word on the line.

I come from the Latin words *sub* plus *portare*, "to carry." _____

I come from the Old English word *threat*, "pressure or oppresion." _____

I come from the Latin word *suspicere*, "to look from below." _____

I come from the German word *schwutsche*, "a long, thin stick." _____

I come from the Old Norse word *stakra*, "to be unsteady." _____

I come from the Latin word *terrificare*, "to frighten." _____

I come from the Old English word *thuruh*, "through." _____

I come from the old German word *takel*, "to take." _____

I come from the Latin word *traditio*, "a handing down or giving over."

_____

I come from the Latin word *territorium*, "the land around a town."

_____

Synonym Chain

Each chain is linked by **synonyms**, or words with similar meanings. Fill in the missing link in each chain with a synonym from the box.

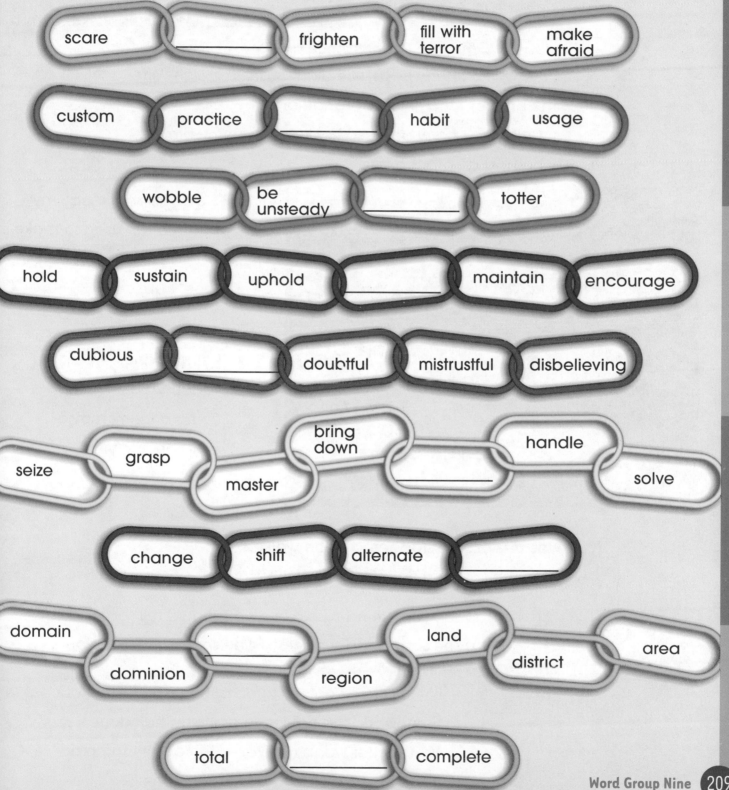

scare — _____ — frighten — fill with terror — make afraid

custom — practice — _____ — habit — usage

wobble — be unsteady — _____ — totter

hold — sustain — uphold — _____ — maintain — encourage

dubious — _____ — doubtful — mistrustful — disbelieving

seize — grasp — master — bring down — _____ — handle — solve

change — shift — alternate — _____

domain — dominion — _____ — region — land — district — area

total — _____ — complete

Antonyms

Draw lines to match each word with its **antonym**, or opposite.

tradition	reassure
terrify	new way
stagger	trusting
suspicious	walk steadily
switch	partial, incomplete
thorough	stay the same

Check the box next to the sentence that makes more sense.

☐ I really like cherry pops, so I didn't want to switch with my brother, who had an orange one.

☐ I really like cherry pops, so I switched with my brother, who had an orange one.

☐ It's a traditional meal; my grandmother used to make it.

☐ It's a traditional meal; I just made it up.

☐ Seeing a ghost would probably be terrifying.

☐ Seeing a funny movie would be terrifying.

☐ He was dizzy, so he staggered as he walked.

☐ He was dizzy, so he didn't stagger at all.

☐ If you see something suspicious, you should tell someone.

☐ If you see something suspicious, you shouldn't tell anyone.

☐ My teacher wants us to do a thorough job on our homework and not leave anything half done.

☐ My teacher wants us to do a thorough job on our homework and leave things half done.

Terra, Terra, Territory

The root **terra-** means "land." Finish the sentences.
Choose from the words in the box. Some are used more than once.

Word Box

extraterrestrial	terrain	territorial
sales territory	terrarium	territory

_____ is another word for a large area of land, a region.

The backyard is my dog's _____, and believe me,

he's very _____.

I planted a little garden in a glass box to make a _____ for my turtle.

The _____ is very rocky.

Sales representatives for the company sell the products in a certain region

of the country. This is called their _____.

_____ means "out of this earth." It is used to describe
creatures who live on other planets, like the alien in the movie *E.T.*

Do you have any space that's your personal territory? _____

Play Ball!

Football is one of our most popular sports. Hundreds of professional athletes play it. Millions of people watch it. In fact, watching the Super Bowl every year with family and friends has become an American tradition. When and how did this sport begin?

A form of football was played thousands of years ago in ancient Greece. Called *harpaston,* the object of this game was to move a ball across a goal line by kicking, throwing, or running with it. Players could be stopped with a tackle. These tackles could be so fierce that the players hit would often stagger when they got up.

Most sports experts agree the American version of football was developed in the 1800s. It was a combination of soccer and an English game called rugby.

Football audiences developed when people became interested in college games. The first official football game was held in 1869 in New Jersey. The Rutgers University team took on the Princeton University team. At last, there were hard, fast rules concerning both team's territory on the field, their time-outs, and other aspects of the game.

Support for and interest in noncollege games was still slow to build. Professional football teams weren't started until 1920. They became the National Football League (NFL) in 1922. Today, professional football's Super Bowl is the most widely watched television event in the world.

Go, team!

Are the following sentences about the passage true or false? Circle **T** or **F** for the correct answer.

The ancient Greeks played a ball game similar to football.	T	F
In the Greek game, no one could be thrown to the ground, and no one ever got hurt.	T	F
College football started in the 20th century.	T	F
American football is a combination of soccer and rugby.	T	F
The first college game took place in New York.	T	F
Football now is part of the fabric of American life, handed down from generation to generation.	T	F
Professional football was popular right from the start.	T	F
Official rules establish field areas that belong to the different teams.	T	F
It took two years for the professional league to be named the National Football League.	T	F

Tiger Territory

Complete this passage about a day in the life of a tiger. Use the words from the box.

Word Box

mischief   support   terrifying   thorough

occasionally   suspicious   territory   threaten   tradition

It's hot and dry in grasslands. This is tiger _____.

One tiger keeps an eye out for anything _____. He

watches for other animals or people who may _____ the big

cat's family. Another tiger rests from the heat and leans against a tree for

_____. All around them, tiger cubs wrestle, nip each other,

and get into _____. When the cubs get too dusty, the mother

tiger grabs them by the back of the neck. She does a _____

job of cleaning the cubs by licking them. _____ one little

cub may escape her notice and go back to playing.

Hunting tigers was a _____ for a long time. Now, there

are not many tigers left. It's _____ to think that this beautiful

animal might die out.

Little Riddles

Finish the rhymes.
Choose from the words in the box.

Word Box

stagger	territory
suspicious	thorough
switch	threaten
tackle	tradition
terrified	

That's the way it's always been done.

For years and years—it's a _____!

To say "walk unsteadily, zig-zag, swagger,"

the word you want to use is _____.

Shift, turn around, use a different kind.

When you _____, you change your mind.

Land, area, your own little place—

_____ is the word for a certain space.

When you start a big project,

_____'s the verb that would be correct.

If anything makes you feel unsafe or unsure,

_____ is the adjective you'd use, for sure.

Whether it's in school or in your neighborhood,

feeling _____ed never feels good.

Scared and frightened, the boy cried and cried.

The adjective to describe him is _____.

Dot all your i's and cross your t's.

A complete and _____ job is sure to please.

Fortunately . . .

These fortune cookies are all missing a word.
Complete each fortune with a word from the box.

© Your dearest wish will come true.

Word Box

support	switch	territory	threaten
suspicious	tackle	thorough	tradition

You will soon _____ a big problem.

Do not be _____ed by your own fear of failure.

Be _____ of people who flatter you too much.

Value the _____ of your family.

Do not underestimate the importance of family _____s.

You will soon venture into new _____.

You are a very _____ reader. (You read this whole fortune, right?)

You might want to consider _____ing brands of toothpaste.

Write your own fortunes, using at least one word from the box in each.

1, 2, 3 Syllables

Draw lines to connect the 2 syllables of these words.

stag	port
sup	ger
tack	ough
thor	en
threat	le

Do the same for these 3- and 4-syllable words.

ter	di	tory
ter	ri	fy
tra	fu	tion
sus	ri	cious
con	pi	sion

Unscramble this 1-syllable word.
It has 6 letters and only 1 vowel!

chitws _____

Alphabetize Away!

Without looking at the dictionary pages, put
these 20 words in alphabetical order.

suspicious _____

switch _____

threaten _____

tradition _____

solution _____

seize _____

tackle _____

terrify _____

territory _____

satisfy _____

represent _____

request _____

scarce _____

stagger _____

support _____

reveal _____

thorough _____

shatter _____

source _____

release _____

Wild-Animal Show

Every animal in this show gets a prize. Fill in the blanks that tell which prize each one gets. Choose from the words in the box.

A wolf that won't stop showing its big teeth: Most _____

A big, angry bear: Most Likely to _____ the Audience

A flamingo wearing high heels: Most Unusual _____

A dog who encourages all the other dogs to do well in the contest:

Most _____ive

A lizard who doesn't make any eye contact and keeps mysteriously

disappearing: Most _____ Behavior

A lion who doesn't want any of the other animals in his area:

Most _____

A friendly, furry, funny rabbit: Most _____ly Pleasing!

Describe an animal that would get the award
Most Likely to Tackle One of the Judges!

_____

_____

Be Thorough!

Thorough means "careful and complete." But it's easy to confuse it with some other words. Complete the sentences. Choose from the words in the box. You have to use one word more than once.

Word Box

thorough	thoughtful
thoroughly	through
thoroughness	throughout
thought	trough

Walk _____ the door and into the house.

You did a very _____ job on your report!

Pigs eat from a _____.

_____ the week, there will be many opportunities to ride my bike.

Someone who is really nice and caring might be called good

_____ and _____.

An idea you get when you are thinking is called a _____.

It was very _____ of you to send me a get-well-soon card.

Please clean the kitchen _____, since it is very messy.

Her _____ in her work impressed her boss.

What was the last thorough job you did? _____

_____

IOU One!

These words are missing their **i**'s, **o**'s, and **u**'s. Fill in the missing vowels.

trad ___ t ___ ___ n

terr ___ fy

s ___ pp ___ rt

s ___ sp ___ c ___ ___ s

sw ___ tch

terr ___ t ___ ry

th ___ r ___ ___ gh

Here are some more words with **o** and **u** together, like **thorough**.
Fill in the **o** and **u**, and read the words aloud.
This vowel combination doesn't always make the same sound!

c ___ ___ ch   tr ___ ___ t

r ___ ___ gh   b ___ ___ nd

t ___ ___ gh   w ___ ___ nd

___ ___ nce   s ___ ___ r

gr ___ ___ ch   bl ___ ___ se

Drip, Drip, Drip!

Dear Mom and Dad,

    You were right: coming to this camp was a great idea . . . except for one thing: rain, rain, rain!

    It has been raining nonstop since I got here. Maybe I should have been suspicious when I first saw the name of the place: Camp Monsoon. Of course, I didn't remember what monsoon meant, so I looked it up in the moldy camp dictionary. "Monsoon: a rainy summer season." You couldn't ask for a more thorough definition of this place!

    We've had to switch our daily plans every day. A long hike through the woods turned into a short hike through the mud. A fun evening at the campfire turned into a 100-yard dash to our tents to avoid a downpour. One camper was terrified of the thunderstorm. I was more worried my tent would leak. The seams threatened to burst under the weight of all this rain. These raindrops are enormous! Even the frogs take cover!

    The counselors say some day the sun will shine . . . but nobody ever gives a date!

        Love,

    Your Soggy Daughter

Dear Soggy Daughter,

Oops! We thought the camp sign-up sheet said Camp Muldoon. Care package with raincoat, boots, and umbrellas is on its way!

Love,

Mom and Dad

Find and underline these words in the passage: **suspicious**, **switch**, **terrified**, **thorough**, and **threatened**. Then rewrite those sentences below, using synonyms for the underlined words.

_____

_____

_____

_____

_____

In what way are the words **terrify** and **threaten** similar?

_____

How might you use the words **stagger** and **support** together in a sentence?

_____

What do you think a person building a house would need a **support** beam for?

_____

What does the term **tackle** mean in football? Does it mean the same thing if you're not talking about football?

_____

Why do you think the House of **Representatives** in Washington, DC, is named that?

_____

Read thse words: **suspect**, **suspicious**, **suspicion**.

Which are nouns? _____ _____

Which is an adjective? _____

Which can be a noun or a verb? _____

Rhyming Riddles

Use words from the box to answer these riddles.

What is it called when you take turns throwing a baseball?

_____ and _____

What do loyal fans do at a baseball game?

_____ the _____

What do you call a book about a piece of land?

_____ of a _____

What do you call a trip you make every year?

A _____ of _____

What do you call food that tastes good but may be poisonous?

_____ but _____

What do you do when you catch someone at football and then laugh?

_____ and _____

What do you call a very carefully made rabbit home?

A _____ _____

Look Carefully!

Circle the word described.

What word means "to endanger"?
threaten   tread   through

Which means "complete"?
through   thorough   throw

Which is a verb?
terrify   terror   territory

Which means "to walk unsteadily"?
stagger   stagnant   stingy

Which is a verb?
satisfy   situation   pacifier

Which means "custom"?
trading   tread   tradition

Which is a verb?
support   supper   supporter

Which means "to knock over"?
trickle   tackle   track

Which is an adjective?
success   suspicious   suspicion

Which means "to change"?
swatch   switch   twitch

It's a Tradition

Tradition comes from the Latin word **traditio**, meaning "a handing down." Complete the sentences below, using words from the box.

Word Box

tradition	traditionally
traditionalist	traditions

Caps and gowns are

_____ worn at graduation ceremonies.

A _____ is someone who believes strongly in doing things the way they have been done in the past.

Another word for **custom** is _____.

My family has many special made-up _____. For instance, every year on your birthday, you have to wear a birthday hat all day!

Match the winter holidays with their traditions.

Kwanzaa	decorating a tree with lights and ornaments
Chinese New Year	putting a black, red, and green *mkeka* (mat) on the table
Christmas	eating moon cakes and watching a dragon parade
Hanukkah	lighting a menorah eight nights in a row
Las Posadas	eating *bunuelos,* fried sugar tortillas, and playing with a piñata

Story Starters

Write the opener for a story by finishing these sentences.

Jaime staggered into the house and yelled, "_____

_____!"

"Something suspicious is going on," Kisha said. "I saw _____

_____."

"Would you switch sandwiches?" Sara asked Tyrone. "Mine is a _____

_____."

Liz finally had a big problem: _____. She tackled

it by _____

_____.

"Um, I don't want to terrify you," Debbie said to Carlos. "But right behind you is a

_____

_____."

Max thoroughly searched the basement for his missing baseball. He found

something unexpected. It was _____

_____.

Dara and her friends have a silly tradition. Every February 1, they _____

_____

Crossword Puzzle

Use the words you learned in Word Groups 8 and 9 to fill in this puzzle.

Across

1. Complete
2. Distrusting
3. A lion fiercely guards his _____.
4. Opposite of to keep a secret

Down

2. Totter
5. Eating turkey on Thanksgiving is a _____.
6. The silence was _____ by a shout.

Word Scramble

Unscramble the words. Then draw lines
to match the **synonyms**.

pportus _____

ackelt _____

witsch _____

netthrea _____

fyirert _____

rawn _____

tempta _____

dloh pu _____

earcs _____

hcgnae _____

Word Group 9 Answer Key

207 support

208 stagger, support, suspicious, switch, tackle, terrify, territory, thorough, threaten, tradition

209 terrify, tradition, stagger, support, suspicious, tackle, switch, territory, thorough

210 radition/new way; terrify/reassure; stagger/walk steadliy; suspicious/trusting; switch/stay the same; thorough/partial, incomplete; first box in each pair should be checked

211 Territory, territory, territorial, terrarium, terrain, sales territory, Extraterrestrial; answers will vary.

212–213 T, F, F, T, F, T, F, T, F

214 territory, suspicious, threaten, support, mischief, thorough, Occasionally, tradition, terrifying

215 tradition, stagger, switch, territory, tackle, suspicious, threaten, terrified, thorough

216 tackle, threaten, suspicious, support, tradition, territory, thorough, switch; answers will vary but should reflect understanding of words' meanings.

217 stag/ger, sup/port, tack/le, thor/ough, threat/en; ter/ri/tory, ter/ri/fy, tra/di/tion, sus/pi/cious; switch

218 release, represent, request, reveal, satisfy, scarce, seize, shatter, solution, source, stagger, support, suspicious, switch, tackle, terrify, territory, thorough, threaten, tradition

219 Threatening, Terrify, Stagger, Support, Suspicious, Territorial, Thorough; answers will vary.

220 through, thorough, trough, Throughout, through, through, thought, thoughtful, thoroughly, thoroughness; answers will vary.

221 tradition, terrify, support, suspicious, switch, territory, thorough; couch, rough, tough, ounce, grouch, trout, bound, wound, sour, blouse

223–223 Answers will vary.

224 Answers will vary; **Nouns:** suspect, suspicion; **Adjective:** suspicious; **Noun or verb:** suspect

225 Switch/pitch, Support/sport, Story/territory, mission/tradition, Delicious/suspicious, Tackle/cackle, thorough/burrow

226 tread, thorough, terrify, stagger, satlsfy, tradition, support, tackle, suspicious, switch

227 traditionally, traditionalist, tradition, traditions; Kwanzaa/putting a black, red and green *mkeka* (mat) on the table, Chinese New Year/eating moon cakes and watching a dragon parade, Christmas/decorating a tree with lights and ornaments, Hanukkah/lighting a menorah eight nights in a row, Las Posadas/eating *bunuelos,* fried sugar tortillas, and playing with a piñata

228 Answers will vary.

229 **See answer at right.**

230 support/hold up, tackle/attempt, switch/change, threaten/warn, terrify/scare

page 229

Dive Into the Dictionary! The guide words at the top of each dictionary page tell you the first and last words on that page.

tread (**tred**)
1. *verb* To walk on, over, or along. *We trod the path toward the beach.*
2. *verb* To press or crush with the feet; to trample. *Don't tread on my feet, please.*
3. *noun* The flat, horizontal part of a step.
4. *noun* The ridges on a car tire or the sole of a shoe that help prevent slipping.
5. If you **tread water,** you swim in one place with your body in a vertical position.
▷ *verb* **treading, trod** (**trod**), **trodden** (**trod**-in)

tri·umph (**trye**-uhmf) *noun* A great victory, success, or achievement. ▷ *verb* **triumph** ▷ *adjective* **triumphant** (trye-**uhm**-fuhnt)

un·ion (**yoon**-yuhn) *noun*
1. An organized group of workers set up to help improve such things as working conditions, wages, and health benefits.
2. The joining together of two or more things or people to form a larger group.
3. the **Union** The United States of America. *The president gave the State of the Union address.*
4. the **Union** The states that remained loyal to the federal government during the Civil War; the North.

ur·gent (**ur**-juhnt) *adjective* If something is **urgent**, it needs very quick or immediate attention. ▷ *noun* **urgency** ▷ *adverb* **urgently**

vast (**vast**) *adjective* Huge in area or extent. *The Sahara is a vast desert.* ▷ **vaster, vastest** ▷ *noun* **vastness** ▷ *adverb* **vastly**

vol·un·teer (*vol*-uhn-**tihr**)
1. *verb* To offer to do a job, usually without pay. ▷ **volunteering, volunteered** ▷ *noun* **volunteer**
2. *adjective* Formed or made up of volunteers, as in *volunteer firefighters.*

wea·ry (**wihr**-ee) *adjective*
1. Very tired, or exhausted. *We were weary after the long trip.*
2. Having little patience or interest; bored. *James grew weary of eating the same lunch every day.*
▷ *adjective* **wearier, weariest** ▷ *noun* **weariness** ▷ *adverb* **wearily**

wis·dom (**wiz**-duhm) *noun* Knowledge, experience, and good judgment.

wreck (**rek**)
1. *verb* To destroy or ruin something. ▷ **wrecking, wrecked**
2. *noun* The remains of something that has been destroyed or damaged. *The divers were searching for the wreck of an ancient ship.*

wring (**ring**) *verb*
1. To squeeze the moisture from wet material by twisting it with both hands. ▷ *noun* **wringer**
2. To get by using force or threats. *The government agents tried to wring a confession from the spy.*

Use one of the 10 words defined above to complete this rhyme.

Whenever help is needed,
one thing is clear:
you should raise your hand

and _____.

Word History

The history of each word is described below. Write the correct word on the line. Choose from the words in the box.

Word Box

tread

triumph

union

urgent

vast

volunteer

weary

wisdom

wreck

wring

I come from the Middle English word *tredel*, step of a stair. _____

I come from the Latin word *triumphus*, "triumph." _____

I come from the Latin word *unus*, "one." _____

I come from the Latin word *urgere*, "to urge." _____

I come from the Latin word *vastus*, "an immense space." _____

I come from the Latin word *voluntas*, "choice." _____

I come from the Middle English word *weri*. _____

I come from the Old English word *wis*, "wise." _____

I come from the Middle English word *wrek*. _____

I come from the Old English word *wringan*, "to turn, or wind." _____

Synonym Skiing

Ski down the **synonym** slope! Draw lines down the ski paths
that have words that are similar to the highlighted ones.

triumph	**urgent**	**vast**	**weary**	**wring**
victory	pressing	great	tired	squeeze
success	imperative	large	fatigued	twist
achievement	insistent	massive	worn out	compress
win	important	huge	exhausted	wrench
				clasp

Antonym Sentences

Use words from the box to rewrite each sentence, giving it the opposite meaning.

Example:

What a terrible defeat!

What a wonderful triumph!

The announcement was unimportant.

_____

The space was small.

_____

I'm energetic when I wake up.

_____

We will stomp along the path.

_____

Sue avoided doing the extra cleanup.

_____

Write about the biggest triumph you ever experienced.

_____

_____

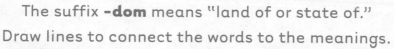

Da-Dom!

The suffix **-dom** means "land of or state of."
Draw lines to connect the words to the meanings.

wisdom	state of being bored
freedom	state of being famous
kingdom	state of being free
boredom	common sense, good judgment
stardom	area controlled by a king

Write about your very own kingdom or queendom. Fill in your name
before **dom**, and describe what your territory would be like.

A Place Called _____dom

_____

_____

_____

_____

Tread Lightly!

Use the words from the box to finish the sentences.

Word Box

downtrodden	tread lightly	treadmill	trod
treading	treading water	treads	

The past tense of **tread** is _____.

A machine you can walk or run on is called a _____.

In a crowd, _____, because you don't want to trample anyone's feet.

We _____ along the nature trail. We didn't step off the path so we wouldn't hurt any plants or wildlife.

_____ are the ridges on the bottom of a shoe that keep you from slipping.

It was beautiful _____ along the mountain path at sunset.

If you stay afloat in water without really swimming, you are _____.

Someone who is _____ feels like they have been walked all over and not treated fairly.

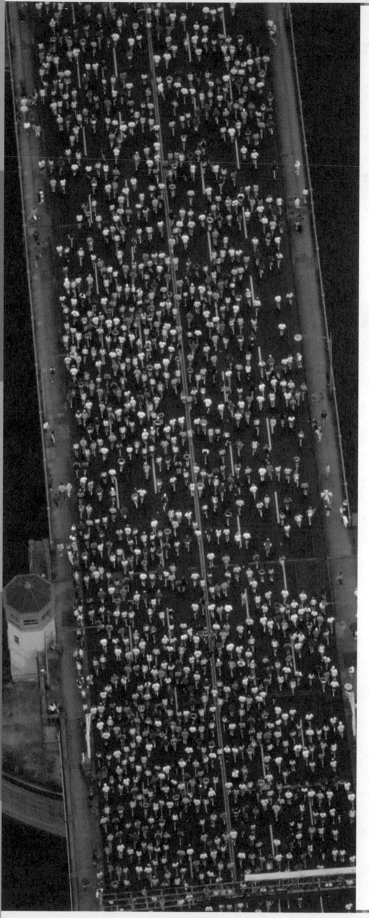

The Long-Distance Runner

The flag is waved.
The contest begins.
It's a race to the finish,
until somebody wins.

The distance is vast.
The miles stretch on.
But the long-distance runners
are already gone.

Some runners tread softly;
some pound on the track.
They strain and they push
to break out of the pack.
Running requires a union
of body and mind,
to keep up the pace
and not fall behind.

The runner feels weary,
his body needs rest.
But the race is a struggle.
The race is a test.

Will there be triumph
or heartbreak and sorrow?
No matter, the runner
can still try tomorrow.

Look in the passage for the words that complete these sentences.
Hint: You have to use one word more than once.

Trod is the past tense of the verb _____, "to step."

Add the suffix **-ant** to _____ to get the adjective form, which means "victorious."

_____ is an adjective describing a runner's feeling.

_____ is a noun with many meanings; the one used here is "combination."

The adjective _____ is a small word, but it means "something of very great size."

Add the suffix **-ness** to _____ to get the noun form, which means "being tired." Careful of the spelling!

Another meaning for _____ is "organized group."

Defeat is a synonym for _____.

Great Triumphs

A **triumph** is a great victory, success, or achievement. Each person in the first column has experienced a great triumph. Match the person to the triumph.

explorer	made an important agreement with a company that helped many workers stay safe
long-distance runner	saved a family from a burning house
911 operator	though weary, finished a marathon
labor-union representative	put through an urgent call that got an ambulance to a sick person just in time
ambulance driver	saw a vast stretch of land that had never before been seen by human eyes
shoe designer	saved people who had been hurt in a car wreck
volunteer firefighter	developed a kind of sneaker with special treads that guarantee the wearer will never slip and fall

United We Stand

You'll see the words **union** and **united** used in words related to government and politics. Why do you suppose this is? Write your answer on the line.

_____

Fill in the blanks with the correct words from the box.

Word Box

United Arab Emirates

Union Jack

United Kingdom

United Nations

United States

The 50 states in America: _____

The union of the countries of England, Scotland, Wales, and Northern Ireland:

_____

An International organization to promote world peace and economic development:

_____

The flag of the United Kingdom: _____

Seven Middle Eastern states unified since the 1970s:

_____

Don't Let ph Fool You!

When put together, **ph** sounds like **f**. Say **triumph** out loud.
Then add **ph** to each word, and read the words aloud!

trium ___ ___ ant   ___ ___ armacy

trium ___ ___ ed   ___ ___ ase

___ ___ one   ___ ___ oenix, Arizona

sap ___ ___ ire   ele ___ ___ ant

___ ___ oto   tro ___ ___ y

In which situation would you NOT feel **triumphant**?
Put a check next to it.

☐ Winning a race.

☐ Winning a game.

☐ Running for the bus and missing it.

☐ Getting 100% on a test.

☐ Doing something you were once scared to do.

Volunteers Needed!

Complete this poster.

Choose from the words in the box.

Word Box

triumph   urgent   volunteer

unite   vast

_____!

_____s Needed!
The School Bake Sale is coming up.
We need people to help sell
a _____
assortment of cakes, cookies, and
other Goodies to raise money
for our school.
If We all _____,
We Will make the Sale
a _____!

What other ideas would you add to this poster to encourage
people to volunteer? List 3 things.

_____

_____

_____

Flags-R-Us

Complete this advertisement for a flag company. Choose from the words in the box.

We _____ all types of flags and flagpoles. We have a

_____ assortment of flags from which to choose. We make state

flags, country flags, and any other kind of flag you want. We'll put your name on a

flag. We'll make a flag for your clubhouse.

We have been in this business for centuries, so we have years of

_____ about flag making.

Our flagpoles are easy to install. You will not become _____

trying to put them in your yard.

Our flags are easy to clean. Just wash in cold water with soap; then

_____ the excess water out and let dry. We can also make

your flags very quickly, if your need is _____.

We're the best flag company there is. We _____ over all our

competition.

We fly our flag high!

Super-Short Stories

Read the beginnings of these very short stories.
Then complete them, using your imagination!

It was a good thing Josh's sneakers had thick treads, because _____

_____.

What a triumph! Katie and Erin finally _____

_____.

"Come quickly!" the explorer called out to his friends. "It's urgent. There is a _____

_____."

The wilderness was so vast the hikers decided to _____

_____.

When Leo volunteered to work at the school tag sale, he never thought _____

_____.

Shakir was weary. He had traveled all the way from _____

_____.

The old woman was full of wisdom. When asked about what was most important

in life, she said, " _____

_____."

"What happened here?" Cody's mom asked. "It's a long story," Cody replied.

"Here's what happened: _____

_____."

Sal was wringing her hands with worry because _____

_____.

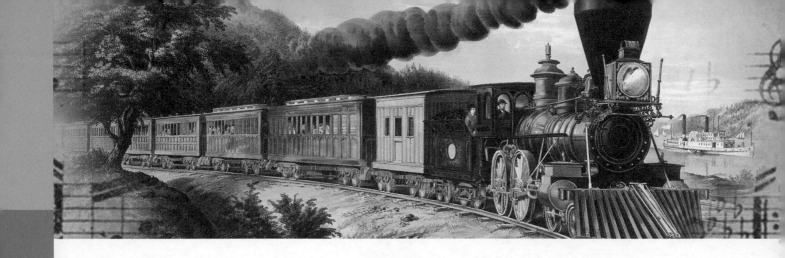

Casey Jones

Have you ever heard of Casey Jones, the legendary train engineer? Casey ran the *Cannonball Express*, the high-speed passenger train. The *Cannonball Express* ran from Chicago to New Orleans, a long route filled with sharp curves and dangerous turns.

One wet, foggy night in April 1900, Casey volunteered to work a double shift. Some doubted his wisdom in taking the job. But Casey needed money to help support his family.

When Casey boarded the *Cannonball Express*, the train was running late. The engineer needed to make up for lost time. He kept his hand on the throttle until the *Cannonball Express* was shooting down the tracks at more than 100 miles per hour. The train company shunted other trains to sidetracks to make way for the thundering *Cannonball*.

The train was only two minutes behind schedule when it approached Vaughan, Mississippi. The *Cannonball Express* rounded a curve, and then Casey Jones saw it: red lights glowing up ahead. That could mean only one thing: another train.

There was another train, stopped on the tracks, unable to move. A train worker shouted an urgent warning to Casey. The *Cannonball* engineer slammed on the the brakes. But there was no way they could stop in time.

"Jump!" Casey Jones ordered.

The *Cannonball*'s other trainmen leaped to safety. But Casey Jones stayed put. The engineer kept his hand on the brakes. He knew if he kept pressing those brakes, they would slow down the train and lessen the impact of the crash.

He was right.

Casey Jones was the only person who died that terrible April night. He stayed on board the *Cannonball Express* to prevent an even greater train wreck. He must have had to wring every ounce of courage he had to remain so steadfast. His bravery and wisdom are now celebrated in story, legend, and song.

Number the sentences below from 1 to 10 to show the order in which things happened in the story.

_____ Casey pushed his train faster and faster to make up for lost time.

_____ A train was stuck on the tracks, right in Casey's way.

_____ Casey stayed on board the *Cannonball Express* to slow the speeding train.

_____ Casey ordered the other trainmen to leap from the train.

_____ Casey offered to work overtime.

_____ Casey Jones got a job driving the *Cannonball Express*.

_____ Casey Jones died.

_____ The *Cannonball Express* approached Vaughan, Mississippi.

_____ A train worked called out to get Casey's immediate attention.

_____ The *Cannonball Express* crashed into the train on the tracks in front of it.

All About Me

Circle **T** or **F** (true or false) to tell about yourself.

I have sneakers with **treads**.	T	F
I have recently felt **triumphant**.	T	F
I have been to three states in the **Union**.	T	F
I have a **vast** collection of something.	T	F
I have done **volunteer** work in the past.	T	F
Right now I feel very **weary**.	T	F
I know someone who has much **wisdom** and life experience.	T	F
I have seen pictures of the **wreck** of the *Titanic*.	T	F
When I worry, I sometimes **wring** my hands.	T	F

Now fill in the bubble next to the answer that tells about you.

If I could do any **volunteer** job, I would
- ○ work in an animal shelter
- ○ feed hungry people
- ○ clean up the streets

If I could have a **vast** collection of anything, I would choose
- ○ CDs
- ○ books
- ○ video games

Pyramid Power

Help build these pyramids.
Fill in the missing bricks.

Word Box

triumph   vast
urgent   weary

1

_____
antonym: **narrow**
synonyms: **immense,
great**

2

_____
antonym: **energetic**
synonyms: **tired,
fatigued**

3

_____
antonym: **defeat**
synonyms: **victory, win**

4

_____
antonym: **unimportant**
synonyms: **pressing,
important**

Syllable Pair-Off

Draw lines to connect the first syllables to the second syllables to make real words. Then use each word in a sentence.

tri	gent
un	dom
ur	umph
wea	ion
wis	ry

_____

_____

_____

_____

_____

1-Syllable Wonders

Unscramble these 1-syllable words.

kwecr _____   dtrea _____

riwng _____   stav _____

Shipshape

Boats from all over the world are docking to be in a contest. Every ship or boat wins a prize in this contest. Complete the name of each prize. Choose from the words in the box.

A boat on which all the sailors are soaking wet: In Most Need of

_____ing Out

A sailboat with a torn, tired-looking sail:

Most _____

A canoe filled with three wise women:

_____ Award

A ship full of people who go all around the world helping others:

Best _____s

A broken, messy barge clearly in need of repair: Biggest _____

Lifeboat that saved a man from drowning: Best Alternative to

_____ing Water

Enormous ship, so big it doesn't fit at the dock:

_____-Deck Award

Boat on which the whole crew really sticks together: Most _____

Yacht on which people play games all day and everyone wins:

Most _____ant

Who Am I?

Read the descriptions. Then write the right word on the line.
Choose from the words in the box.

Word Box

tread	union	vast	weary	wreck
triumph	urgent	volunteer	wisdom	wring

I have 1 syllable and only 1 vowel.
I start with **w**. I can be a noun or a verb. _____

Same as above clue, but I can only be a verb! _____

I have 1 syllable and I begin with **v**. _____

I have the most syllables of any word on the list. _____

I rhyme with **bread**.
I am a verb or a noun. _____

I have 2 syllables and a silent **p**. _____

I have 3 vowels, and I am a noun. _____

I have 2 syllables, and the stress is on the first.
I begin with **u**. _____

I have 2 syllables.
I mean "tired." _____

I have 2 syllables.
I begin with **w**. _____

Little Riddles

Complete the riddles. Choose from the words in the box.

What did the workers get after they finished cleaning up after the storm?

Three _____s, for the _____s

How do you feel if you are tired and sad?

_____ and _____

What do you call a victory of organized workers?

A _____ _____

What is another way to say "quick and wide"?

_____ and _____

What do you call good advice from your mother?

_____ from _____

What is another way to say "destroy the porch"?

_____ the _____

What is another way to say "to keep walking"?

_____ _____

Crossword Puzzle

Use the words you learned in Word Group 10 to fill in this puzzle.

Across

1. I had to _____ the water from my wet shirt.

2. She _____ for duty in the Army.

3. Opposite of divorce

4. Step

Down

2. Immense

5. An SOS is an _____ message.

6. In the final leg of the race, he WOL and won!

7. Clear thinking

8. A _____ ball knocked over the building.

9. Opposite of energetic

Word Group 10 Answer Key

232 volunteer

233 tread, triumph, union, urgent, vast, volunteer, weary, wisdom, wreck, wring

234 **triumph:** victory, success, achievement, win; **urgent:** pressing, imperative, insistent, important; **vast:** great, large, massive, huge; **weary:** tired, fatigued, worn out, exhausted; **wring:** squeeze, twist, compress, wrench, clasp

235 Answers will vary but should include these words in this order: urgent, vast, weary, tread lightly, volunteer, triumph.

236 wisdom/common sense, good judgment; freedom/state of being free; kingdom/area controlled by a king; boredom/state of being bored; stardom/state of being famous; answers will vary.

237 trod, treadmill, tread lightly, trod, Treads, treading, treading water, downtrodden

238–239 tread, triumph, Weary, Union, vast, weary, union, triumph

240 explorer/saw a vast stretch of land that had never before been seen by human eyes; long-distance runner/though weary, finished a marathon; 911 operator/put through an urgent call that got an ambulance to a sick person just in time; labor-union representative/made an important agreement with a company that helped many workers stay safe; ambulance driver/saved people who had been hurt in a car wreck; shoe designer/developed a kind of sneaker with special treads that guarantee the wearer will never slip and fall; volunteer firefighter/saved a family from a burning house

241 Answers will vary; United States, United Kingdom, United Nations, Union Jack, United Arab Emirates

242 triumphant, triumphed, phone, sapphire, photo, pharmacy, phase, Phoenix, elephant, trophy; running for the bus and missing it

243 Urgent, Volunteer, vast, unite, triumph; answers will vary.

244 manufacture, vast, wisdom, weary, wring, urgent, triumph

245 Answers will vary.

246–247 3, 5, 8, 7, 2, 1, 9, 4, 6, 10

248 Answers will vary.

249 1. vast, 2. weary, 3. triumph, 4. urgent

250 tri/umph, un/ion, ur/gent, wea/ry, wis/dom; wreck, wring, tread, vast

251 Wring, Volunteer, Tread, Triumph, Weary, Wisdom, Wreck, Vast, United

252 wreck, wring, vast, volunteer, tread, triumph, union, urgent, weary, wisdom

253 cheers/volunteers, Weary/teary, union/win, Fast/vast, Wisdom/mom, Wreck/deck, Tread/ahead

254–255 **See answer at right.**

pages 254–255